George – a Müller's Boy

To Val

Happy Christmas (2001)

Thanks for all the support
and being such a
great friend.

Lots of love
Debs x

George. E. Collett.

**George Müller - founder of the
Müller Homes, Bristol**

George – a Müller's Boy

George Collett

paternoster
Lifestyle

First published in 2001 by Paternoster Lifestyle

07 06 05 04 03 02 01   7 6 5 4 3 2 1

Paternoster Lifestyle is an imprint of Paternoster Publishing,
PO Box 300, Carlisle, Cumbria, CA3 0QS, UK
and Paternoster Publishing USA
PO Box 1047, Waynesboro, GA 30830-2047
www.paternoster-publishing.com

British Library Cataloguing in Publication Data

A catalogue record for this book is available from the British
Library

ISBN 1-85078-414-0

Cover design by Campsie
Printed in Great Britain by
Cox and Wyman, Reading, Berkshire

Contents

Foreword

'I didn't really enjoy it much but it was a wonderful foundation for the rest of my life.' I hear this so often from boys and girls who spent their formative years in the Müller Orphan Homes at Ashley Down in Bristol. Most of us cannot imagine ourselves in the same situation as those boys and girls who had lost one or both of their parents. Müller's Homes provided Christian care at just the right time for them. It was not the sort of care that many children experience through being part of a loving small family unit. This was care on a much larger scale with strict discipline, lots of rules, little privacy and hard work. But so many children who were brought up in Müller's will affirm that the upbringing they experienced has served them well in their later life. Many have gone on to be hardworking, law abiding and upright members of society. And the impact that this shared life together had on them enabled them, in the midst of whatever personal tragedy had brought them to Müller's, to feel part of a family – the Müller family.

But there was another ingredient – that was their exposure to the Christian faith through daily teaching, Christian services and the testimony of many Christian men and women who had devoted their life's work to serving God through child care. Many of the Müller family can identify the influence that Müller's had on their lives spiritually either because they decided to follow Jesus Christ whilst in the Homes or, as a result of remembering what they had been taught there, they became Christians later in their lives.

However, it was not just the care and teaching that they received in the Homes that was a challenge to faith but also the knowledge that the Homes of which they were a part were founded by a man whose faith in and commitment to God was known the world over. The influence of George Müller's life of prayer and faith, his trust in God and his commitment to serve God is a powerful story. This was a man who was converted from a somewhat dissolute lifestyle to a man who trusted that God would meet his every need and who, without ever asking anyone except God through prayer, was given (at today's prices) between £75m to £100m. If ever there was someone whose life and faith was a challenge to us and a model for the lives of young boys and girls, it was George Müller's life and faith.

And that was true of the young boy sharing George Müller's Christian name who found himself at Müller's somewhat bewildered and lost. George Collett's upbringing in Müller's Homes has been a powerful influence at every point in his life – as an orphan and then a teacher in the Homes, in the services, as a missionary, as a church leader and preacher, counsellor and friend. Müller's was where he discovered many things – friendship, foundational life-skills, and faith, often through hard and difficult experiences. But there is this thread that runs through George's life – a passion for people and a passion for God and that the one might know the other.

As you read through these pages, you will find a larger-than-life character whose life seems to have been more than usually filled with challenging experiences. Here is a story which is well documented and observed, at times exciting and always interesting. George's memory for details, events, conversations, is well known to his friends. But there is something more in this story than a good biography. This man was and still is a Müller's boy – and it shows.

Julian Marsh
Chief Executive
The George Müller Foundation
Bristol
March 2001

If you would like more information about George Müller or about the Foundation we invite you to write to:

The Chief Executive, The George Müller Foundation, Müller House, 7 Cotham Park, Bristol, BS6 6DA

or e-mail us at: admin@Müller's.org
or ring: 0117 9245001
or go to our web site at: www.Müller's.org

Acknowledgements

I wish to acknowledge with gratitude Julian Marsh's active support and encouragement throughout. His confidence in me has been an inspiration.

Sue Carleton put my work on disk and printed it with amazing speed and accuracy in the midst of a very busy schedule. I am indebted to her for her time spent and for her patience, perseverance and cheerful tolerance.

I am grateful also to Roger Steer for his interest, encouragement and helpful suggestions at an early stage of the work.

Some years ago Ron Ainger, a technician at City of Bristol College (based in the former Müller's Homes) borrowed one of my manuscripts, typed, printed and bound a hardback copy in red, with gold lettering. It was an inspiration to me at that time to persevere with my work.

My wife, Ruth, has assisted me, first by editing the material of my original book (not published) and then, knowing the events of my life better than anyone, by putting this manuscript in order and getting it ready for submission to the publisher. I believe that without her it would not have reached completion for some time to come.

Finally, I want to thank those who have prayed for me, especially my friends at Thornbury Baptist Church. Their hidden work is most valuable. The book has been bathed in prayer, my own and others, from the start, and it is God Himself who has given strength to complete it.

George Collett
April 2001

Prologue

Everyone's story is unique. So why should I bother to chronicle mine? Perhaps you won't ask why when you have read the story. You will have gained some insight into the kind of inexplicable behaviour that humans seem to indulge in.

The story could embarrass some people and not least the author. He did not invent the happenings that are recorded but he was a very interested participant. When he appears it is not always as the blue-eyed wonder that he was in childhood, or the more battered version that he is now, but as the boy, the teenager, the young man.

I have waited many years to record the events known only to me, firstly because I have been too busy to find the time to write and secondly because of my concern for those involved in the story and for their relations. Now I feel the time has come to recall the events before I grow too old to remember them. Nothing is written in a spirit of malice. I write from a desire to speak truthfully about those whose lives touched mine in the Providence of God.

I aim to be objective without being dull, and truthful without being unkind. Different readers will draw different conclusions perhaps as varied as the people who read this. Don't be too harsh in your judgements of those concerned who all did their best according to their light. If I knew as much about the experiences of my forebears as I know about my own, I would perhaps understand better and be more ready to excuse their seeming inconsistencies.

I hope that, as a result of my own unusual experiences, I may be charitable to those who acted sometimes so strangely and irrationally towards me. The sobering thought comes that we too are being observed by our succeeding generation and that they are making their own judgements, which we hope will err on the side of leniency, and that they will take into account our frailties and the circumstances that have shaped and governed our lives.

Introduction

My two sisters and I were just three of the hundreds of boys and girls who passed through the Müller Homes on Ashley Down in Bristol during more than 160 years of institutional care given to over 18,500 children. We may all have looked similar, but each was an individual, as evidenced when we meet at the reunion each September on the Saturday nearest the 27th, Mr Müller's birthday.

'So where are they all now?' Well, during 160-plus years many of them have, of course, already died. Our children, grand- and great-grandchildren come from all over the United Kingdom and the world to revisit the place of our upbringing. Some do not come back for various reasons. Some have unhappy memories, some are very sentimental and some hardly remember their childhood.

'I cannot remember most things that happened to me as a child,' said Stan, a resident in the 1940s and 50s. 'I suppose I was lucky, I won a scholarship to go to the Technical College at 13+. Then I left and went into a job. I was in lodgings with a Christian couple from the Baptist Church. I met my wife there and we have three children and eight grandchildren. I have just retired after 46 years in the same firm. I was a director/manager when I left. Our family number 16 at present. We will grow when the grandchildren become parents.'

Some former orphans/residents do not marry, but if Stan is representative of his generation, then there are many hundreds of thousands of their children and families alive and their number is growing year by year.

I had a very different experience. God's plan for my life did not turn out so smoothly or seem so well ordered. But then 'God knows what he is doing,' I told one friend who criticised God for all that had happened to him. 'I can't imagine anyone going up to Him and saying, "You made a mistake with me! You didn't understand me, did you? Couldn't you have done better for me?" '

Stan asked me, 'When did you begin to realise God has a plan for your life?' I replied, 'In some ways I've always known it. People I met after leaving Müller's used to call me lucky as things always seemed to turn out well for me in the end.'

A deep impression of God's protection and planning was made on me in the swimming pool at Ashley Down where I had a very narrow escape. This was not the only one, as you will see later. Much of my life was linked to the Müller experience and especially to the teaching and example that George and Mary Müller passed on in their lives, especially about living a life of faith and obedience to God and His Word.

It was, I believe, in obedience to His word to me that I have written this book. I woke one night with a sentence from the book of Jeremiah on my mind: 'Write in a book all the words I have spoken to you,' and later, 'Take a large scroll and write on it with an ordinary pen.' I found these last words were from Isaiah, so I followed them and took up my pen.

Beginnings

I can scarcely remember ever living in an 'ordinary' home. Since birth I either lived in other people's homes or in children's homes. I was born the third child and only son of a Welsh father and a German mother in the city of Cologne. The year was 1923 and I was registered as a Natural-Born British Subject in the Rhine Army Supply Depot. It was not a good time to be born in Germany of a British father because of the rise of the Hitler regime. Threats to British ex-servicemen persuaded some to return to England; others disappeared. My father knew of some who were supposedly pushed into acid vats in the factories where they were employed.

We lived in a large house on Nueser Vall (North Wall) – No. 9 – with the River Rhine at right angles to our road. My grandfather was a manager in ICI and I was told he travelled all over Europe 'buying forests'. My father was later employed in ICI after completing 22 years in the British Army.

My memories of Cologne are brief but pleasant. A blue stretch of water – the Rhine. An Alsatian dog called Jim, pulling a dog cart in the back garden. My mother sitting in a chair at the back of the house. I didn't know then that she was ill with tuberculosis, from which she died soon after we came to England. She had given birth to three children in three years. Mother needed help as she and grandmother were too frail to care for our household of seven. As she was an only child servants had to be employed. There was no difficulty financially and there were plenty of able young women to help with the housework.

Grandpa Bremke was a big kindly man who was a deeply sincere Christian. Grandmother was a small woman but memories of her are indistinct. He spoke English fluently, she hardly at all. I was bilingual for about five years, but had gradually forgotten almost all my German by the age of ten. In acquiring English I developed a stutter as I had to drop the use of German gutturals.

My first adventure was connected with an electric van which rumbled down our side street. There was nothing remarkable about it until, one day, I mounted the step-in cab in the absence of the delivery man. I had evidently learned how to operate some of the controls by observation. All went well and I was on my way to the main road, the railings and the river beyond, when a flurry of shouting and activity arrested a rather exciting trip, which might have ended an apparently promising career. I was returned to my indignant family and dealt with in a thoroughly Germanic fashion.

I was in trouble on another occasion due to the fact that I evidently possessed initiative. Jim, the Alsatian dog, was without water and I, feeling sorry for him, decided in the kindness of my heart to supply it – personally! This was a simple process for a little boy and also a relief for a pressing problem that I happened to have at that moment. The dog bent down to slake his thirst and then I was discovered. The awful fact that came to light warranted further chastisement, but I was surprised to note that the dog escaped scot-free!

I was about three when Hitler's party was coming into power. Inflation was stamped out and the Nazis were firing national pride. An ex-soldier friend of father's was threatened that if he didn't get out he would be pushed into the chemical vats. He refused so he disappeared. My father did not wait to get the same message. He decided we must leave for England. It must have been a terrible wrench for my parents and grandparents, but soon we were on the boat on our way to England and South Wales.

Britain was in the middle of the Depression at that time. In the Rhondda Valley families of miners were 'on the soup kitchens' with a piece of bread and bowl of soup for each member of the family. We could only stay with my aunt and her family in a small miner's house in Pontypridd for a very short time. Lottie, my mother, was too ill to do much. Uncle was a coal miner, but unemployed as the mines were shut. The house became unbearably overcrowded so we went to London in the hope of my father finding work. Mother's health was deteriorating and she had to go into hospital. We were in a couple of rooms in Harlesden and my father had a temporary job nearby. He paid for someone to care for us, now 3, 4 and 5 years old, and was evidently subsidised by money from his father-in-law Herr Ernst Bremke in Germany. Our Welsh family was in deep poverty.

One day father returned from the factory to find that our carers had abandoned us, taking everything of value, and we were left alone, hungry, cold and crying. There were two homes for motherless children in West London, so as a matter of urgency he went to their headquarters and Smith's agreed to take us in temporarily. I was separated from my sisters, who went into the girls' home while I went into the boys' home. I never remember visiting their home, and I never saw my mother again. It was when I learnt to read the word 'motherless' that I began to realise that she must have died. It was about 60 years later that I learnt that she died in hospital a few miles away from where I was.

Children in our family were not told these things. I was never taken to visit her and have only that vague impression of her sitting against a white wall in Cologne. I remembered our dog called Jim and my father who was also called Jim. He signed himself D. L. Collett. His real name was Demetri Lacudi because of his Mediterranean mother.

There were about 30 boys at Smith's Homes, also a matron, a nurse and a cook. There was a constant stream of young girls who came and left at intervals. We were dressed in clothes supplied by our families. I had plenty of 'German' clothes, and also had one or two visits from my grandparents in the eight years I lived in Ealing. Except for living in this very large house – now a solicitor's office, and the only remaining house on that part of Uxbridge Road – we lived like other families, going to local schools and churches, to the park and to Ealing Common with others in the Home, often in charge of a nurse or an older boy.

We slept five or six in a bedroom and lived communally. Discipline was more noticeable here than in our home in Germany. I grew up with it, so I didn't notice it too much. My father came to take us out about once a month. I envied my friend Leslie Chalk, as his dad had a motorbike and sidecar. He sat on the pillion and his sisters in the sidecar with their hats back to front.

Small Fish – Big Pond
(How I came to Müller's)

The Depression continued and one week miners marched to London along the A4 through Ealing to Buckingham Palace. They camped on Ealing Common and the whole neighbourhood turned out to give them jugs of tea and food. My father's Army pension was 75 pence a week, plus some other earnings from temporary work. Having to pay for our keep, he soon fell behind with his payments, as you can imagine. Sometimes he could not afford to take us out on the Saturday, as it meant tram fares and tea at Lyons Corner House, plus pennies for roundabouts and ice creams.

Smith's Homes spent some time discussing with him what they should do about his three growing children and his increasing debts. The only solution that presented itself was an orphanage called Müller's, in Bristol, near Wales. (For a long time I thought it was 'Mothers' Homes' because of the notice outside our 'Home for Motherless Boys'.) It took my father 15 years to pay off his debts to Smith's Homes after we left. Müller's had the attraction that it was free, which was a miracle. People in the local churches assured my father, the matron and Smith's that it was true. References were given and forms sent to father to fill in. I have photocopies of them all, including my school report written in 1933.

Soon we were heading West for a cluster of huge buildings housing over 1000 children. Once there had been 2050 plus staff and workers.

As an active, lively boy I had been in some scrapes at Smith's, and once the angry cook had shouted, 'George Collett you'll end up in prison one day!' Some of our cooks were very angry people and, until I was old enough to go to school, I had evidently tested their patience to the limit. One day, it was said, I threw a knife at the cook. The facts are not clear, but I threw something. It was evidently a knife. It missed and stuck in the door. Things were pretty uncomfortable for me as a result, and I gained the distinct impression that my action would lead to some dreadful penalty – I could only think of prison – so the day I was told I was leaving the Home I thought that was where I was going. My suitcase was packed and early morning goodbyes said, especially to my friend Leslie Chalk, and then we were off to meet my sisters.

Paddington was huge and very noisy with its steam trains. My father was on tenterhooks, not at all like his usual self. And so we came to Müller's, Bristol, and sat in the waiting room of what looked like a prison to me.

The buildings stretched almost as far as my eyes could see. Long lines of children marched along with teachers (they seemed to my imaginative mind to be guards).

The boys had close-cropped hair and the girls had pigtails. They looked very old-fashioned, whereas my sisters and I had ordinary clothes and looked like ordinary children. In Ealing we had gone to local schools, churches, parks and shops. All that was to stop now and we would walk out in such long lines that the Police had to be informed, to see us over main roads. A woman came to fetch us after my father had quickly kissed us goodbye, muttering something which sounded like 'I'll see you soon'. (It was four years later, when I was leaving Müller's, that I saw him next.) A Matron came and took my sisters and told me another lady was coming for me soon.

We went up a long drive to the Boys' Wing. She took me into a large space full of cupboards and long tables. Then I had to have a bath and all my clothes were taken away. I was now fitted, from the skin outward, with different clothes – three sets of them – and was told I would be No. 23 from now on. In a room off the main one were four women, sewing and darning. They spoke to me with their 'Bristle' accents and were very kind to me. During my four years there they were a kind of lifeline to the outside world. We had a lot in common except for the cigs and the gin! Years later, when I returned at 25 years of age, I still felt a bond with them – and the other outsiders who worked around the place.

Now came the culture shock – to meet the other boys. I was one of the youngest and smallest of them and felt like a sideshow at the circus. Boys crowded round me like a swarm of bees and fired questions at me with bewildering rapidity.

'Can you sing in tune?' and 'Can you do mental arithmetic?' Because if I could not I was going to get

THIS and a number of hard-looking fists were stuck under my nose, too close for comfort. I assured them that I could do both very easily. I tried to put on a brave face and didn't cry, but I could hardly understand a word they said. I found that they burst out laughing when I tried to answer their questions and that one of them was busy 'taking me off' to the huge delight of the rest. Next a barber came along and my hair was cut to what the boys called a 'Bicky' (short for biscuit). It was cropped short and from now on I was the same, or at least I looked the same, as all the others.

I lay in bed that night in a cavernous dormitory with about 50 other boys and held on to my London bus tickets. Later, when it was nearly dark, one of the staff came round and found me still awake. A kindly word and a pat on the head, and I soon fell asleep.

I was not in prison. I was in Müller's Homes, Bristol, and strange to tell, I still have connections with them all these years later.

Why the Bell Rang

Discipline now took on a different meaning. Instead of 30 boys there were now more than 300 in this house alone, with 50 in each dormitory. Everything was on a large scale. Queues of children marched about the place to wash, read, play or eat. 'Stop running' was the order. 'Get into line Collett', 'Lead on', 'Stop there'. 'All stand; sit down; kneel down; get up.' These were not shouted, often just a movement of the hand, a nod, even a look, and hundreds of boys would obey. Sometimes there was some freedom of choice.

When getting ready for bed each was numbered – I was No. 23; Collett No. 23. The boy next to me gave me a dig in the ribs and pushed me in the right direction. We undressed at night or dressed in the morning and stood at the foot of our beds. We got into bed when told – unless we wanted (said kindly) to kneel and pray. I may have done sometimes, I often wanted to, but it was hard unless you were 'genuine', because the boys would scoff at you. 'Call yourself a Christian?' and then they would produce very damning evidence.

There were five different houses. For Babies and Infants No. 1, Infants No. 2, Boys No. 4 and Girls

Nos. 3 and 5. Infants upwards were divided into Boys and Girls, and Juniors and Seniors.

Domestic girls aged 14 to 17, who had left school, had their own wings and dormitories. Houses Nos. 3, 4 and 5 were of almost the same plan, except that they were East-West or North-South, mirror fashion. In my four years as a boy I never remember going into the girls' wings except to see my sisters once a month on a Monday afternoon. Parents and family could also visit, but my father never did come. He explained later that he thought it would upset us. I left when I was 14 and my sisters were 17 – but that's another chapter.

Older children who came into the Homes were put into the charge of a boy or girl to show us the ropes. They explained why the bell rang, for school, meals, etc. and guided us into the way to do everything. 'Getting into your line' when moving from place to place to eat, wash, going to a service or one of the many things that happened in a child's life in a large institution.

Everyday life was very much routine and I soon became used to lining up to go to meals. I came to know my place in the queue, and who was behind and in front of me. As a 'freshie' I was tolerated if I made a mistake, but soon I found that the pecking order very much applied. I was being 'put in my place'. As I grew older and bigger, so I moved 'up'. Only my bed, No. 23, stayed the same.

Every boy had a job. My first one was with a bucket of hot water, Izal, soap, scrubbing brush and flannel. I joined a gang of others with a monitor in charge and was 'led out' to clean the toilets –

outside in the playground. A certain number of
cubicles, basins or urinals were given to me to
clean, with the threat to 'do them properly or else'.
I received a weekly credit to my account for doing
my job properly. Every boy had an account with a
basic weekly deposit of money (pence) added or
taken away for duties done. If done well then promotion came along regularly to whatever job was
suitable. The senior master would line us boys up
with the monitor in charge of our department and
choose who would move or stay.

As boys and girls were coming into the Homes
and leaving them on a regular basis aged 14 (or
17 for the girls) so the moves constantly changed
what we did. It was in fact quite slow and at first
there was no hope of change until you had done
your work well. By the age of 13 I had done most
of the 'jobs' at ground level, cleaning, keeping
shoes and clothes in order, putting out meal-
places, helping in the kitchen – in fact all the
chores. Now I was considered suitable for a
monitor's post.

There were trial periods when I was put in
charge of a class, if the master (teacher) had to be
absent or came in after school started, sometimes
because of illness, or family problems at their own
homes. Most of the masters were old boys, and
the mistresses old girls. They had been through
'the school' and had sat in the desks and slept in the
same beds as ourselves. Each master had their own
special responsibility, first for their school class,
then for the jobs to be done, and then extra things
like games, library, and inspection of shoes. They

kept their eyes open for likely boys to be monitors to replace those leaving.

The three most important jobs were the passage boys, the sitting room boys and the messenger/errand boys. One of them was the 'chief', the head of the school. They were chosen early so that they were not due to leave too soon. I never reached this position because I was caught 'pinching' oranges from the huge baskets that came at harvest time. I think most of us were guilty, but I walked into the trap set up and paid the penalty – six of the best and demotion – but not for very long. I did not split on the others (that would have made my life a misery) so I was dubbed 'Prince of Orange' by my fellow errand-boys, who shared their spoils with me.

My name went in the Punishment Book in the cupboard where the canes were kept in the masters' sitting room. This was the hub of the building, and 12 years later I was admitted as an assistant master into the privilege of being on the staff. Some years later when I became a housemaster my name was on the other side of the Punishment Book when I had discovered two big boys putting a smaller boy's head down the lavatory pan.

As an errand boy I was one of the very few who went into Bristol. We had cap and cape and an errand basket carried on the left-hand side. We were supposed to walk there and back to take and collect orders to various business offices. As one who had lived 'outside' until 10 years of age, I soon found a way to stuff my cap and cape into the basket, once out of sight of the Homes, put my tie in my pocket and hop on a bus. I was often given a free ride. Then having done my errands I would go into Woolworths, or a store where there was a café, and have fish and chips and a drink, being careful to wash and rinse my mouth before hopping back on the bus to pick up my uniform. I was never found out and certainly never told even my best friends. So you see, these freshies need to be carefully watched.

Shortly after arriving at Müller's, I was surprised to hear that there were going to be 'parties' every Friday. Also that there were going to be cakes for tea. This meant that every Thursday evening there was to be a lot of cleaning and scrubbing of floors. Shoes were cleaned and polished, black in winter and brown for sandals in summer.

All the week there were boys doing Swedish club drill and swinging on bars or balancing on forms. At least one evening a week a master would keep us in for singing practice; songs I had never heard like 'Brook, said a little stream whither are you going?' or 'Little Sir Echo how do you do?' This one turned into disaster the first time we did it in public. The 'echo' boys were out of sight in the classroom off the main schoolroom. We got stage fright and a fit of the giggles. This turned in the end to helpless laughter and the experiment was abandoned. After this we 'echoes' were kept in the public eye and not very popular with the other boys. We were all kept in one fine evening to do extra practising.

As a boy in Smith's Homes for the motherless in Ealing, I had been to many parties and we had our own at the Home. Now at 10 I found that there was another meaning to the word 'party'. Like many English words you have to know the context. The 'party' was a group of visitors that came to see round the senior boys' house every Friday afternoon from about 2.30 to 4.00 p.m. All the five homes on Ashley Down were open to visitors on one day of the week, Monday to Friday. Each home had their own programme: songs, recitations and 'exercises'. Girls did 'things for wenches' with skipping ropes, hoops and tambourines, I think. I don't remember seeing them, but have seen pictures. At holiday times – theirs not ours – we had huge crowds, sometimes coach-loads, Christmas, Easter and Harvest time, mainly from Sunday schools, churches and sometimes from overseas. It was a bit of a chore for us, but guaranteed frequent spring-cleaning.

We didn't like being stared at by other 'outside' children, though as it happens, my future wife was one of them. Her family had had to leave Southern Ireland in a hurry, due to the trouble there and had bought a home near Müller's. She tells me she always watched one particular boy, at the end of a certain row, and my place was there. She was six! The Master on duty was there with his pitch pipe and metronome, and look out if you were caught misbehaving, like shaking a fist or making a face. On wet days we marched around the town in what is now the St Paul's district. We went in a long line in twos with a master or two and with a prefect at intervals along the crocodile-like line of children. Kids in the streets, often shoeless and scruffy, shouted at us, 'Yer, look at them orfans' and made rude signs at us. We replied, but very carefully, 'Come over here and we'll give you a thick ear.' Would you believe it, in time some of them did. Then they were given clothes, shoes, regular meals and they were on 'our' side!

When the teachers wanted boys to recite or sing a solo verse I would volunteer – at first. Then I found I was very unpopular with the other boys. 'Collett is swanking', or 'a show-off' was what I got, sometimes with a push. At this time I began to stutter. I had a slight German accent on some words and was learning to speak English. I'd got over it in London, but now with a large number of boys and visitors present I got stage fright and also some jeering from my schoolmates. Even today, if I think about some words, I want to stutter. Then I gradually learned to think ahead and if possible find another word.

Whenever my grandfather wrote to me from Germany he addressed me as 'Dear Ernst', but this was not to be for long. One day, when we were in school, and the senior master was sitting up in his desk way above us, a special messenger came into the schoolroom and tip-toed up to the desk where he was sitting. In his hand he had a black-edged envelope. The master opened it carefully, read it and looked around the rows of faces. With a feeling of certainty I felt his eye rest on me.

He dismissed the messenger and then called me up to his desk in the gallery that ran along one end of the room. In his hand he held the letter. He was faced with a difficult task. He too had been a boy in the Homes. He was married to a girl who was also a former Orphan and they had one child, a little girl. He had to harden himself to many years of human problems, his own and those of hundreds of others. Discipline was the answer. This was what made life orderly and bearable. Years in the First World War in the British Army strengthened the orderly pattern of discipline already laid down in childhood. It also gave him the smoking habit which was a source of wonder to us. We could always smell his 'baccy' when we came over to the schoolroom from our house across the road. Now he must break the sad news to this new boy standing at his right hand. Better be brief, firm, and put in something helpful. He dismissed the rest of the class and stood with the letter in one hand and placed the other kindly on my shoulder.

'George, I have some rather sad news for you. Your grandfather in Germany has passed away. He has gone to Heaven to be with God. Do you know what that means?'

'Yes sir.'

'Good. Well now you can go out to play with the other boys.'

I went out and mechanically answered the inevitable questions. They were quite kind and did not presume upon my private thoughts. Later that evening after tea I went out into the playground. It was dark. The stars were shining brightly in the winter sky. I looked up and remembered the Master's words, 'Gone to be with God.' It was true. I knew it and felt it very definitely as the tears streamed silently down my cheeks. I was

comforted. I went into the warm playroom to play
with my friends.

One source of special interest were the preachers
who came to conduct our services in the week and
twice on Sundays. Also our own teachers and staff.
Copying them was one of our hobbies. One
preacher had a whistle when he spoke, especially
when giving out a hymn number. 'Number three
hundred and (whistle) sixty (whistle) six.'
Unfortunately I had practised this and when asked
to choose a hymn or chorus, had unwittingly
copied him. It was not well received and I got my
come-uppance. Even today at reunions we give
very recognisable performances of the preachers
and teachers whom we knew so well many years
ago. When I returned as a housemaster at 25 I was
very conscious of all this and tried to avoid any
'funny' mannerisms.

Craft lessons in progress in a Müller home

In at the Deep End

I have swum in many different places around the world and loved it.

When my father brought my two sisters and me to the Müller Homes in Bristol in 1933 I was 10 and they were 11 and 12.

The Matron took me across the Ashley Down Road to the Junior Boys' Wing. We went up a long drive. As we passed a long glassed-roof building she said, 'That's our swimming pool. Can you swim, George?'

'No miss,' I said, 'but I've been in the sea at Bognor and Southend.'

'Then you'll soon learn, I expect,' she said.

The swimming bath was an advanced feature of the Homes. It was a gift from an anonymous donor who asked that only two conditions be observed: (1) that he should remain anonymous, and (2) that he should have a key to see the children enjoying themselves. This was told to us by the Senior Master when this very old man had been watching the swimming and some boys had made fun of him.

It was in this same pool that I came within a gasp of losing my life. I looked forward to swimming. I'd never heard of a school or home that had a swimming pool before – not even in London. Among the

clothes laid out for me was a swimsuit. My number
– 23 – was sewn into it. The following week we
marched with our teacher to the swimming bath.
'The best in Bristol, if not in the West of England,'
said Col. Woodcock, Head of the Baths Committee.

I had to stay in the shallow end with the non-
swimmers and the smaller boys. The Head of
Juniors took us and was very strict but firm with
his discipline – calling everyone 'Tommy'.

A few months later I moved up to the senior
wing, although not yet 11. I was one of the youngest
and newest boys. I was called a 'dinkie' and a
'freshie'.

The teachers in the senior schools took us swimming at regular times each week. There were about
1000 children in the Homes then. I have always
been grateful that I learned to swim and have
taught many others to dive and swim – but it
wasn't always like this. During the summer I was
allowed to start swimming lessons. These were
conducted by a master who had not been in the
Homes himself as a boy; neither had he any training as a teacher. He taught woodwork and I
remember him as being loud and somewhat unpredictable.

The method of starting beginners was to line
them up along the shallow end of the bath and
encourage them to jump in. I was still a beginner,
without any fear, then, of the water and I looked
forward to learning to swim. I went to the deep end
to watch the life-saving group. The instructor was
the master with a loud flamboyant manner. The six
boys on my side of the bath were to jump in and

shout 'Help!' The six boys on the other side were to swim across and life-save them.

While I was so engrossed somebody came along behind me, and evidently could not resist the temptation to push me in. I gave a yell and disappeared in 6 ft of water, as I was quite unable to swim. But of course I was only one of several boys thrashing about in the deep end shouting 'Help!'

I, the non-swimmer, in dire need of assistance was the only one without a boy to rescue me! In due time all the others were towed across the bath and I was still feebly thrashing about trying to call help and taking great gulps of water.

At last the instructor noticed me... he dived in and in a moment brought me up to the surface... but now my troubles began! I presume he did not realise I was a non-swimmer as he proceeded to almost complete the drowning process. He towed me round the deep-end, using me as a demonstration of what to do with a struggling swimmer.

Every time I struggled or shouted he ducked me under, and when I'd been round the circuit of the deep-end I was pushed in the general direction of the shallow-end and told not to fool around.

By now I had ceased to struggle and was only capable of faintly gulping in water. I sank blissfully to the bottom and, after the terror and turmoil of the last few minutes, I found it peaceful and strangely warm, like being in bed and sinking into the clothes. Then suddenly a strange cold feeling came over me. I felt a great weight holding me down. It was as though I was standing in cold wet rags in a place of absolute misery. The noises above me faded and now in front of me was what seemed to be an immense wall and a door partly open. I seemed irresistibly drawn to the door. There was a warmth and a magnetism that drew me on. I found myself at the threshold. The terror of the past minutes was over now. There was a new and exciting prospect before me.

My impression was of a brilliant, scintillating world that was calling me irresistibly on through that open door.

There were brightly coloured birds and insects darting about and varied hues of flowers in profusion everywhere. Beyond that there were other, indefinable attractions, but I seemed short-sighted and no clear impression was left on my mind. I was moving slowly and surely into that garden. I wanted to go into it. I felt I had one foot over the threshold and in a moment I would stand in all the warmth and beauty of that place and be surrounded by the splendours I had dimly perceived. It was the final revelation and realisation of all that my mind or body could conceive.

At this crucial moment I felt a giant hand dragging me back and, though I might struggle, and struggle hard, I was not able to advance one inch or to maintain the ground gained towards that opening vista.

Someone had evidently noticed my downward progress to the bottom of the bath and I was now being rescued for real. I found myself in a grey, cold world, my head being forced between my drawn-up knees as I sat on the side of the bath. Water was pouring out of my mouth and nose and seemed to be coming up from my stomach. I was later hauled to my feet fairly briskly and taken to the changing rooms where I somehow managed to dress. Good training and discipline came to my aid and the warm sunshine of the terrace outside helped to restore me.

It took me a year before I could go into the swimming bath again. I used to sit on the edge with my legs dangling until my fear was overcome. Later on I taught many people to swim and dive and have had so much fun. I have also assisted in a number of real-life rescues in baths, canal and river and gained the bronze medallion for life-saving while at College.

I have never actually felt afraid of death itself, though I realised that later I was not as ready to die as I had been on that day and in fact was never sure that I would go to heaven until, when I was 25, I became a follower of Jesus Christ. Fear of the pain which may be associated with dying is very real to me but, alongside it, I always carry images of warmth and colour of that brilliant world that I glimpsed through the open door, and since that day I have never doubted that there is a heaven and a life after death.

Sex Education?

'What sort of sex education did you have?' is a question I have only been asked in private discussions after giving a public talk on my upbringing in children's homes in London and Bristol. As the youngest of three children and the only boy, I was always conscious that I was a boy and therefore that I was different from my sisters and I was aware of the 'family'. My first three years were lived in changing family patterns in Germany, Wales and London.

From being part of a family of three children I became one of about 30 boys. We were all ages from 3 to 16 and went to the local schools. We dressed in clothes provided by our families. Mine were often from Germany – as were the cards and presents I received until my Grandfather died in 1934. As boys we bathed together as in any family. Bath nights, usually on Friday, were a time for water games – if left to ourselves, as children do all over the world. There was no mention of anything sexual from those who cared for us. I was the youngest boy and therefore less developed than the others.

We went to mixed Infant and Junior Church schools (C of E). At 10 I was taken to Bristol. There were then a thousand children in care in the huge

Homes on Ashley Down. Once there had been over 2050 children. Our ages ranged from a few weeks to 17 years. We were all in uniform with men and women teachers, matrons and other male and female staff. Most of the men were married with children and had themselves been boys in the Homes. The women were single and also mostly former residents. Other women employed, but not directly with the children, came in from 'outside' and were mostly married.

The male married staff lived outside and some were married to former orphan girls. We children had a good basic education, but there was never any mention of 'sex'. In those days sex described gender, and was not a 'doing' word. I had lived in the County of Middlesex. That was my only memory of the word. I understood that people made love, but it was not called 'having sex' in those days.

The boys and girls lived almost completely separate lives on the same huge site. Brothers and sisters met once a month under supervision of the masters and mistresses. This was also the day that their remaining family outside could visit, from 2 to 4 p.m. on 'Visiting Day'. There was no mixing of boys and girls except on one day every year, the Annual Picnic and Sports day on Purdown.

As boys left at 14 years of age, the majority of us were immature. We had a saying, 'Girls are wenches,' which was said with a sneer and in a condescending manner. The children lived communally in huge dormitories of about 50. Most of the children had been admitted when infants or juniors. Very few had experience of the outside world. They knew a lot about each other, and those who brought them up, but almost nothing about the outside world. I came into the Homes four months after my 10th birthday. My two older sisters, 11 and 12, were also called outsiders and freshies.

We had lived 'normal' lives. Of course girls are much more mature than boys of a similar age simply on biological grounds. The girls did not leave the Homes until they were 17, but I gather that their sex education was little better than ours. I was the first to leave the Homes as I was 14 in 1937. My sisters were older, then 15 and 16 years. They left in 1938 and 1939 when they reached 17.

It was not only at Müller's that children lacked sex education. At that time society in general still looked on sex as something of a taboo subject and children were not taught the facts of life. Many went into adult life having to discover for themselves.

Some of the carers were better than others in conveying attitudes to the children, but one, an 'outsider', told the girls that 'if you kissed a man you could have a baby'. This is an extreme case, of course, but generally speaking as far as the girls are concerned I have never discussed the subject, though I'm told that any teaching they had was rather vague and obscure. I married an 'outsider'. She has been very good for me.

When the girls were 14 they moved from the School to the Domestic Department. Some of them were drafted into the Nursery and Infants Department and into the Juniors. Some went on to train as nurses and some as teachers. A number also came back to Ashley Down and only if they were professing Christians were employed to teach or nurse the children. A small number of these then went on to marry former orphan boys and so left to set up their own families, while some husbands continued a life-time of service in the Orphan Homes.

As children our lives were very busy with every hour of the day time-tabled. Schooling occupied a large part of our time, along with meals, cleaning, and all the chores about the place. Playtime was usually a boisterous interval 'if we behaved ourselves' and if not, then we would have detention – being kept in/or homework, or to practice singing in preparation for the weekly visiting days.

We also had swimming in the warmer weather, and had a weekly bath night. How do you bath 300 boys? We had a huge washroom with basins around the walls and a sunken footbath filled by overhead showers where we boys soaped ourselves after an initial wetting. Then the master-in-charge would turn on the shower – hopefully warm – to rinse us off. This was done to 10–12 boys at a time. There was no place for false modesty. Thursday night was our bath time as we had visitors on Fridays.

During my four years as a boy I only remember one boy who was different from the rest. He was more developed, but although some poked fun at him, he never took offence and so it never really became an issue. It may have hurt him, but I still remember him and the sympathy I felt for him when they teased him. I think he was given the nickname 'Daddy' as his voice had also begun to break.

Only in my last year did I find out that this mixing together annually between the boys and girls
gave rise to stories of amazing exploits, none of
which were possible when about 1000 children and
dozens of adults were having an outing in some
large sloping fields. There was a copse and quite a
few large trees, and evidently this fed the imagina-
tions of some romantic boys and girls. It came, I
suspect, mainly from the 'wenches' who had seen
us from afar – or on the visitor's day. The nearest
that I could ever imagine to romance was pushing
each other on the swings set up on an old oak tree.
The boys were generally much more interested in
the games, the cricket match, and when they tried
to launch a hot air balloon. Then of course, dear to
every boy's heart was the 'grub' – lemonade, pork
pies and ice cream – all free. Also some sweets and
fruit in huge quantities. 'Girls were all right – as
long as they gave you some goodies' was, I'm
afraid, most boys' attitude.

Partying

Quite apart, though, from the regular Friday parties, we did have some real parties, as you will see.

Christmas parties were huge affairs. The school-room walls were covered with patterns made of coloured paper, mostly purple I seem to remember, and with a lot of words – texts from the Bible. The rooms were so big that ordinary decorations weren't used in the 1930s. We boys and girls started practising carols and recitations for our pro-grammes for the visiting public. Very large sweet jars began to appear and we were allowed to spend our pocket money plus some extra allowances when the master responsible was on duty. Jobs, schooling and all the other daily things continued but now an air of excitement grew.

We looked forward to parcels coming and a room was set aside to store them until they were handed out. To have a parcel waiting for you was the great thing of the day. How big was it? What did it look like? Where did it come from? Guessing and hoping brought spice into our well-regulated lives. Almost prophetically I guessed my father had sent me a fountain pen and propelling pencil set. It was true and so I was very happy when the big day came for me to open mine. Also some pocket money – for 'lollies' which I could swap with my friends.

My best friend was John Gelder. He was, like me, a 'freshie'. Coming from London I spotted that his name in backslang was 'Redleg'. Then came rehearsals for the party night. Desks with seats attached were cleared to the sides and if necessary piled up. The floor was washed and polished – by us, with trousers rolled up and bare feet like sailors on the old sailing ships – practice for when I would go to sea in the Second World War just a few years later. We lined up in groups and joined hands. On a signal we would sing and move around the schoolroom in various patterns. I didn't know any of the songs, but most of the other boys had known them since their infant school days. 'The big ship sails through alley, alley oh', 'Sing A B C D E F G' and then when finished forwards, reversing it to 'Sing Z Y X and W V.' I can't remember the sequence now, as I couldn't then, because of the way we had to manoeuvre still holding hands and going into reverse to unwind.

There were more exciting games: stir the bucket with a mop, touch someone and race back to the bucket. In the real party we chose anyone from the visitors or others who were game for a bit of fun.

One of the younger teachers was in charge and with a whistle to command could keep the party games going. Children, staff and visitors numbered hundreds. The most hilarious and dangerous group were 'the preachers'. They were best at making fools of themselves. All the rest of the year they were solemn, but it did their message good when we saw them enjoying the fun. The preachers came with their families and were quite a surprise, as we had no idea that there was a 'human' side to them. We had favourite preachers and discussed which one we would like to be 'converted' by. My favourite was a young couple who went out as Missionaries from the Baptist Church in Ealing. They were Bible Class leaders. One went to China – the woman, and the other to Africa. The Vicar of one of our local churches in Ealing was the Rev. George Summerhays. He was formerly a missionary in Central Africa and was very kind to me when we attended his church. At Smith's Homes, Ealing, like Müller's, we were welcome at any church.

I was converted for real through the influence of my teacher at Müller's and a friend of his who were members of the same local church. Both had families and they were good 'sports'. But that happened about 11 years later, after I had left Müller's.

After the party games were over the visitors left. We had some party food and they went off to supper – except for the staff on duty who went later when the children were in their dorms. The monitors were put in charge but all were soon fast asleep.

It was at such a party as this, after I became a Christian and was now sports-master, that I met and fell in love with Ruth, now my wife since 1954. I courted her for a few years while she trained at the London Foot Hospital and then while I was training as a schoolteacher in St Paul's College, Cheltenham. The games I had learned as a boy, both in Ealing and at Müller's, proved very useful for many years in churches where we've been members, in schools and in various out-of-school clubs that I've run over the years, also in holiday camps and Bible camps in Central Africa.

Right through my boyhood and youth, I was greatly impressed by the fact that Christians did enjoy themselves and had good fun. I always knew that I wasn't a Christian in those days, and was often ashamed secretly by those things that I discovered outside the Christian community. Even though I seemed to enjoy them at the time, I knew deep down that they were a sham, and they brought no real joy. However, I could MC games and have great times without the shadow of doubt creeping into my thoughts. Later, I became like a child, making a completely fresh start with my new-found Christian faith. I could learn how to be a sports-master and how to organise games for every occasion for others to enjoy. Like those games of old I had a lot to learn, but I knew the actions, the words and the songs.

I had gone through years of practice, learning and enjoyment. At the age of 25, after the war was over, I committed my life to Christ, and entered a New World. I had also the thrill of finding a partner who was, I believed, God's choice for me. Ruth (Mary Ruth) was a wonderful discovery to me. It was more difficult to convince her of God's choice, but then we had that priceless treasure of love and romance. We were engaged for a couple of years, and then at our wedding invited family, friends and staff and two children from Müller's Homes to share our happiness and joy at our wedding and reception.

However, many things had to happen between Müller days and this exciting event.

It Was Like This

At most games I was not very adept. I was short-sighted and glasses were eventually prescribed for me. They were horrible owlish kind of things that would only serve to subject me to ridicule. I never wore them unless it was unavoidable. Only when I was about 19 did I go back to them when I discovered I could not see the wonders of the world from the deck of a ship. The boys played a rather brutal form of cricket, which consisted of bowling the cork ball at the head of the unfortunate batsman. Coming off the asphalt in the yard, the ball went like a rocket. Miraculously no one was seriously injured, but as a result I studiously avoided all cricket games. It was the same with football. There was little refinement about the play and indeed both games when played on the field were played on such an acute slope that the results were bizarre to say the least, unless allowance could be accurately made for the degree of deflection experienced once a ball had touched the ground. Later I was to use that slope to distinct advantage.

Reading was my great love. We were allowed a book every so often from a small selection held by the Senior Teacher. I always chose my book according to its thickness. I read the History of the Wars of the Indian Mutinies, and a number of omnibus books. I was also keen on board games, draughts, snakes and ladders and such others that came our way.

We played all the usual children's games well documented by the Opies. We also had a number of our own. One was called 'Hidey on the Side'. This was played in the playground and in the playroom. One team lined up in the playroom near the door and their opponents were outside. One of those in the yard would then dash in and try to catch the inside team before they reached the far wall. Another great favourite was 'Strong Horses'. In this team game the horses made backs while their opponents ran and jumped onto them trying to make them break down by sheer weight. If the runners fell off or touched the ground after jumping they changed places. If the 'horses' were strong enough to hold them they became the riders. Although this is reckoned as a dangerous game today, we did not have any serious accidents that I can recall. We were very strict about keeping the rules and seeing that 'they' did too.

Judge and Jury was a long and rather complicated game. There were two sides and enough pieces of paper for one side. These had all the officers of the court, the witnesses and the criminal written on them. The opposing team's 'Judge' threw all the papers in the air and then they scrambled for their papers. The new 'Judge' had to guess which one was the accused. If he was wrong he was made the criminal. The guilty person always met the justice due for his crimes.

We also did Swedish Club Drill and the boys taught this to each other. Younger boys did dumb-bell exercises and there was a lot of horizontal bar work done on the apparatus in the playroom. All this was really rehearsal for the visitors that came each week throughout the year to see the children and hear them sing and to be entertained by the skill at mental arithmetic, recitations, sketches and various physical activities by the different age groups. The girls did skipping and exercises with hoops.

Christmas was the big occasion. This took months of preparation and practice. Hundreds of local children came to see us with their parents or their church groups or even by themselves. Some were in the habit of making sly remarks at us as they sat on the side. We were not slow in answering or in returning the abuse. They called these 'parties' and as a new boy I naturally thought of games, good food and fun. I was to be sadly disillusioned. The parties were sheer hard work and drudgery for us. Later as a Master I discovered that they were no picnic for the staff either. Everything had to be scrupulously clean everywhere. Every boy and girl had to be as bright as a new pin by the appointed hour. Before we actually saw the visitors there was a rehearsal.

Messengers would come and inform the Master of the numbers of visitors and their progress around the dormitories, kitchens, dining rooms and the Prayer Room and then finally that they were 'on the way'.

On special occasions there was more than one party and literally hundreds came, but on other days a few self-conscious visitors would have to face hundreds of boys or girls who still had to run through their repertoire. We sometimes had Swiss rolls for tea on the visiting days, which were on Friday afternoon in our case.

The Homes were self-supporting in most ways. The incredible story of how they started and have been maintained for nearly 140 years has been told by such people as Dr A.T. Pierson, Professor A. Rendle-Short and Mrs Garfield. Almost £6,000,000 has been sent to the Homes in answer to prayer alone, and never has a single penny been asked for by anyone responsible for the running of the Homes. Naturally these things had a profound effect on my life, once I became a Christian, and undoubtedly on the lives of many of the 18,500 children that have been in the care of Müller's Homes during all those years.

We had our own school, maintenance men, gardeners, bakers, and boiler-men. There were infirmaries on the top floors of most Houses with matrons and nurses in charge, also some very attractive probationer nurses. Older girls helped with some of the domestic duties in the infirmaries and in the infant and nursery departments. Evidently Mr Müller was criticised in the mid-1800s for keeping children at school too long and for 'educating them above their stations'. We had a sound elementary education, both boys and girls until 14 and then the girls left school to do domestic work in the different departments to help run the homes. Some became pupil teachers or probationer nurses or went into other forms of in-service training.

Doctors and dentists visited the children regularly and when required. We dreaded the dentist most of all. I am sure he could never have perpetrated a fraction of the brutalities credited to him. I had to line up for his attentions one dreadful morning. Sister Petherick was in charge.

She was a great wonder to us all. Strict and jolly, lining us up like soldiers, which she often exhorted us to be. She bustled about in her blue and white stiffly starched uniform with the imposing cap standing at attention on her head and her beautiful silver buckled belt gleaming about her waist. Her cuffs too were always spotless. She was ideally suited to us lads. Jolly, full of fun and able to smell out a 'shammer' a mile off. Her treatment might seem rather Spartan by today's standards, but she was effective and well loved by us all.

The clothes worn by the children did not change fashion very often. In the 1930s we wore Norfolk jackets, grey shirts and shorts with long stockings and shoes. I forget the exact colours of the ties, but I think they had a red stripe on them. We also wore grey caps and had blue capes for rainy days. We had grey pullovers for cold weather. This was our 'best' winter wear and it was of good quality and style. We also had a second best set of clothes and day clothes. Of course we were all dressed exactly alike so there was no mistake about where we came from. When clothes needed repair they were done in the workrooms where the sewing ladies were overseen by the sewing matrons. The shoes and sandals were sent to outside repairers and 'daps' or plimsolls were only worn until fit to be discarded.

Each of the masters had an area of special responsibility. We knew that when a certain master came on duty he would have shoe inspection, or clothes checked or pocket money and fines dealt with or sweets sold. Hair, nails, teeth and brushes and combs all had regular checks. The masters were also our schoolteachers and when we were assigned to a class on entering the Senior Boys, we invariably had that teacher for the whole four years and were taught in almost every subject by the same teacher. There was a long time ahead to learn about your pupils if you were a teacher or your teacher if you were a child. I count myself fortunate to have had an excellent teacher who was a fine Christian and a man of great integrity. He was strict but painstakingly fair. He had a dry sense of humour that took time to appreciate. Later I was to work with him as my senior colleague when I started in childcare and education.

There were plenty of personality clashes in a place as big as our's, but there were plenty of others to turn to if you couldn't get on with someone.

The advent of duty days could make the world of difference to our lives. All of the masters, except one, we could predict as to how they would react to pretty well every known circumstance. The exception was the only 'outsider' among the masters. All the others were themselves former orphans and we knew quite a lot about the outline of their boyhood days, which were so similar to our own.

All who aspired to the exalted office of Teacher were thoroughly vetted and the Directors had to be assured that they were people of personal faith and sound in every way. Occasionally some slipped through the net or became disenchanted. It was an exacting task done by a band of women and men for the whole of their lives and among thousands of needy children.

Whether a child was in the Homes for a few years or for the maximum 17 years the day inevitably dawned when they 'left'. This meant, and still means to many today, that they left home, school, family and friends. Their total environment was changed, and at that difficult and turbulent time of life which we now call 'teenage'. For the boy ready to leave, dressed in new clothes, hair allowed a little longer and 'smarmed' with Brilliantine, the last day in the old surroundings arrived. All the preparations, the fitting out in outside shops and the unaccustomed choosing of things that there had never been any choice about before. Then the talking in the dorms after lights out and all the speculations, rumours and stories that were rampant and finally the fitful sleep disturbed by dreams of the great 'outside'.

A special breakfast was prepared for the 'leaver' and the boys who carried his trunk of clothes to Ashley Hill Station. They were called the 'trunkers'. Poor fellow! Having eaten hardly a crumb of his breakfast and after a restless night with all the build-up to this great day, suddenly he finds it all slipping away behind him. Some things and some people he will never forget. Most he will never meet again. Now he is following the master responsible for 'taking him away'.

The journey may be as far as Newcastle and then the master and boy will part when he is handed over to the care of those to be responsible for him. There's a lot of choking down of tears and swallowing as with tremendously mixed feelings they walk down the terrace, along Ashley Down Road and down Station Road, which takes him out into the great unknown.

Some went to employers, some to relatives, but not many others outside these folks. Who would lightly take on the responsibility for a 14-year-old boy? Many went to farms. Wales was quite near. Some were apprenticed to tailors, printers and the like. Some lived to inherit their employer's business and even married into the family. The sort of work they were going to determined the choice of clothes contained in their tin trunks. Those going to farms had lots of boots and shiny leather leggings. I'm sure that some chose their kind of work because of the clothes. They would subsequently change their jobs for more valid reasons.

Decisions

My own case was the exception. I had ambitions to stay and be a teacher, but although I made some half-hearted confessions of Christian faith, I was in fact undecided, although leaning very much toward the Christian way of life. I had been close to that decisive moment called conversion on a number of occasions but had never actually clinched the matter. So I was ineligible to apply and in any case I doubt that my record would have commended me had there been a vacancy.

What would happen to me when my turn came to leave? I did not want to go onto a farm. My father had never been to see me. What things were like with him I had not the faintest idea. I loved him and regarded him as my childhood hero, but he had become a remote, legendary figure far removed from my present situation. He had slipped away four years earlier without a goodbye and on a half-lie. I felt vague, intangible feelings that I can now partly define as insecurity and a loss of basic trust.

Now here I was, a Müller's Boy, in Bristol and due to leave in six months' time. My father was a widower living on a tiny long-service pension with no prospects of a job. He had a room in a large house on the Blackfriars Road and in it was everything he needed to cook, eat and sleep. He shared a bathroom and toilet with all the other tenants in the house, which was on four floors including the basement. How would I fit into this tiny place after 12 years of huge houses and hundreds of children and staff?

One of the junior schoolteachers was a cub master in a local cub pack. His group scout leader came to the Homes occasionally and socialised with us. He was a very tall, thin man with an unusually loud laugh. One evening he came into the schoolroom where I was sitting knitting my 'going away' socks. Every boy had to do three pairs before leaving, either in blue or brown wool. I was happy to do this as I could read a book at the same time. I was due to leave after April 19th on my 14th birthday. I was hopeless at turning the heels and finishing off, so I did plain and purl legs in exchange for other boys who did heels for me.

I was suddenly aware of this stranger in the schoolroom who had come alongside me and was admiring my work. He was a giant of a man to us lads and had an infectious laugh and a hearty and boisterous manner. This could become irritating, as I was to discover much later, especially under adverse circumstances.

From this day on the whole course of my life suddenly took a new and wholly unexpected turn. He spoke to me and asked if I could knit him a pair of Scout socks. He would supply the wool. I agreed to do this.

Now this man began to visit fairly regularly to see his friend and so came to bring me wool and to chat with me. He worked for a local evening news-paper. I told him I was keen to become a reporter. Gradually he got information from me about my father and his name and address. He asked me if I would like to stay in Bristol and learn to become a reporter.

He wrote to my father, telling him that I was interested in a journalistic career and that he was able to help me achieve my ambition. Nothing of this was mentioned to people at the Homes. Eventually he visited my father in London, who told him that it was 'up to George'.

This was an unusual situation, I discovered years later, but an interview was arranged between the Scoutmaster, the Directors and the masters. They said it was my father's responsibility and, despite warnings from my schoolteachers, that is how it happened. Their counsel was over-ruled possibly because of my father's legal right to determine his son's future, and possibly due to the persuasiveness of my mentor.

I was told by my friend that my father had said he was unable to have me as he was renting one room and struggling hard to pay off the debts incurred while we were in Ealing. My father came down from London. I was handed over to him by the directors and then he asked me again if I still wanted to go with this family. The Scout Leader was single and about 35 years old. He said the local Secondary Modern School had agreed to take me for a year and then he'd booked a place for me to go to a commercial college to learn shorthand and typing. It was all so simple.

I went to the station to see my father off after he'd signed all the necessary papers. We had a cup of tea before the train was due. Then we stood rather awkwardly around until he boarded his carriage. As the last signals were being given I went to kiss him goodbye. He pushed me aside rather brusquely and said, 'You're a big boy now.'

He then stepped up into the train, closed the door and the flags were waved, whistles blown and slowly the train puffed out of the station leaving a rather bewildered and hurt young lad looking after it.

Had I done right? Why was my father hurt when it seemed that I had done what was best to help my father and what would at the same time achieve my own ambitions?

However, I realise now that he too was hurt because I had chosen to stay. I understood from this man that my father could not have me as there was nowhere for me to live and he could not do much for me. When I did go back to London after about 18 months he found lodgings for me with a family off Sloane Square, but there was not much time to pursue these hurts and reflections as we had to get back home.

It was soon evident that all was not well in my benefactor's home. There was an indefinable air of tension that one can sometimes detect when visiting a house where there are deep underlying problems. The atmosphere was bad. I had visited their home a number of times before. They were strict people but quite kind to me.

As the meal progressed there were a number of interruptions as they kept going out and there were sounds of a quarrel going on. I was assured 'everything would be all right'. Here I was after all the months of preparation, having left my friends, my school, my home, everything I had known for the past four years and now I was in the eye of a storm. I was so tired from all the excitement, emotion, conflicting things happening that I could no longer keep my eyes open. I'd been awake before the crack of dawn and now it was past 10 o'clock.

I was shown up to a huge bedroom with a double bed and old fashioned furniture and then had to unpack my new clothes, etc., and stumble down and back from the bathroom. I was alone. As I crept into this huge bed, my eyes hardly open, I heard a door open downstairs and a voice saying, 'Charity begins at home.' I left the following morning and he started finding lodgings for me with various Scout families.

He was an impetuous man, but with the best of intentions. He acted very ill-advisedly and had to learn by experience to overcome the problems that his impetuous enthusiasm had created. There was nothing sinister in the man as far as I can remember. Later I knew the Scouts that he had charge of and there was never a breath of scandal about his morals. You can usually get the truth from the boys if any such scandal exists.

Later he went into childcare and was much more effective in fulfilling his ambitions. He died while in that capacity. Perhaps it was a deep need for a paternal relationship that led him into the experiences that involved me. He saw in me a ready-made son. What he didn't see were the built-in problems that every child carries with them that can only be resolved satisfactorily in a stable family situation. This he could not supply. His venture was doomed from the start and he was glad when it was finally resolved. So was I, but that was not to be the end of my troubles, only another chapter.

Müller boys watching County Cricket

A Cup of Tea, Sir?'

Within a day or two of leaving Müller's Homes I found myself lodging in Kennington Avenue, where the back garden joined the orphanage's potato ground on the side of House No. 1. Every autumn the senior boys spent some weeks digging up the potato crop. The masters and boys seemed to enjoy it, but I hated it. They treated it like a holiday. It was time out from school, but to me it was hard labour. The other boys in my class were mostly brought up there since infanthood. They had looked forward to it, but at 10 I dreaded it: the mud, the digging and sorting out potatoes from the stalks.

Gardeners brought huge baskets and supplied us with all the digging tools. They were jolly and there was some backchat going on. The job was easy for them driving around in a van with gangs of boys doing the work. Some of them smoked: that was different and seemed rather wicked. In the 1930s the link between smoking and lung cancer was not known. When we could, some of us copied them out on our own back yard. We used old cabbage leaves and toilet paper. The paper came from old Müller's Report magazines. A few years later after I had left the sea, I found that the price of cigarettes was so dear that I realised that they were only made of similar things, old leaves and toilet paper! The experience of us boys sitting spluttering and coughing on the backyard cured me. Why pay for all that agony? That was many years ago and the money has been better spent, and my own health guarded.

One good thing from the potato digging was the bonfires. We loved making them, and besides, some potatoes got cooked in them. They were often burnt almost to a cinder, but boys are always hungry. The masters, remembering their own days in the school, turned a blind eye. Some had been in the First World War as soldiers, just as I was at sea in the Second.

So in September 1937 I was living in one of those houses bordering the potato field. I remember the day I had 'outside' clothes on, and had left only a short time before. The children, all boys, had gone to school, their parents to work, and here I was bored to death by myself. I waved to the master on duty and asked him if I could get him some tea and toast? This was what I had done for some months as a 'sitting room boy', before leaving.

'Thank you, George,' one of them said. This surprised me as I had always been called 'Collett'. But it was said kindly. So I toasted and buttered the bread and took it down to the bottom of the garden with a hot cup of tea on a tray. I wonder what all my former 'residents' thought. One of the staff did enquire if the parents had given me permission and politely refused.

As I passed it over the wall I knew I was wrong to hand out food which did not belong to me and which would severely deplete my landlady's supplies. I felt uncomfortable and my conscience was stirred. Through this man I was eventually to become a Christian and he was a wise counsellor and a great friend to me until he died many years later. Mr Müller's influence was working in his life and through him and his wife, both former orphans, I learned not only the principles of Christian living but also the practice. To turn away the offer of a cup of tea and plate of toast on a day like this was a real test, and to me an example.

Some years later when I was home on leave and eventually when my war service (and eight medals later) was over, he often invited me and my girl out to tea, to Müller's Christmas parties and to church. They also invited other former orphans, and they were an influence on all of us. We had seen their lives as staff, as a family and as church members.

Through this one man the complete course of my life was changed. I know it was a great encouragement to them when I wrote and told them that I had changed and now loved the Lord Jesus and wanted to serve him always. They lived to see my life unfold as I joined the staff at Müller's, then, after teacher training, taught in local schools and later managed mission schools in Central Africa, before finally returning to England to work in the church and community. George Müller's' faith was passed on to me through them, and we try to pass it on to the next generation.

Into the Wide World

Once I was outside the Homes I began to feel a surge of new life and a battery of new ideas and experiences hit me.

I went for an interview at the Newspaper Office, but evidently the swan was a goose. As a result I was sent back to school. I enjoyed school, had one or two fights with good results and made some good friends. I fell in love. She was dark-haired with a shy smile and started me on the road to romance with a cake made in cookery class. I suffered the agonies of juvenile love. All the horseplay, the shy moments, the waiting about to meet by accident. I saw her every day in class but she seemed a difficult girl to get to know. For some time she was my ideal but when we met 10 years later the magic was gone and only the memories lingered on.

After leaving school I went to Commercial College, as it was felt I should learn shorthand and typewriting. I spent a whole three months wasting my time, with about four other lads, as the instructors concentrated on the girls in the class and left us to ourselves. By this time I was lodging with the widowed mother of a Sea Scout in our troop, so I was kitted out and made a full member of the troop.

I had a new bike and went for long cycle rides at weekends, with friends from the Scout Troop, until the time when we acquired a derelict barge. We had a number of other boats such as a whaler, dinghies, canoes and other craft, but now we were to have a new HQ on the river alongside Bristol Bridge. Later we moved the barge up under the old City Wall. We also acquired a new Skipper with the HQ. He was to assist me in a wonderful way before long. We thought to christen him in the river, but decided against it after we met him. He started our gatherings with prayer and soon the Scouts were telling each other to cut out the language when 'Skip' was about. He was an ex-Royal Navy man and a real sailor. He was also an expert Morse signaller and knew his seamanship thoroughly. I learnt a great deal from him that proved useful, in life as well as at sea.

Now that I'd left school for the third time and was 15 years old it was decided that I should earn my living. I applied for a job in an Estate Agent's Office and was taken on, but had to supply my own bicycle and trousers should they be torn by a dog, but as compensation, I was to receive a 'percentage' on any property I let or sold. What a joke! This never happened as I was made to disappear when a customer came in sight.

Sometimes I was sent to collect rents from tenants. These usually failed to produce any results. The women who answered the doors were more than a match for me. They told me heart-rending tales, which I absolutely believed, and sent me away without the rent. My boss would get really cross with me, though I couldn't understand why. I would start to tell him the harrowing tale, but he would explode into wrathful indignation, telling me he had heard that story a hundred times. It was all an enigma to me.

Up for Adoption

When my second landlady needed extra room the Scout Group Leader took me to the slums of Bristol to see a couple who were going to 'treat me as though I were their son'. I was told I was very lucky that they'd agreed to have me. I didn't want to go, but the Scoutmaster had evidently lost patience with this difficult boy that he had so foolishly taken on

This couple's son had recently been killed in a cycle accident and they were prepared to take full responsibility for me and to adopt me. Here was a simple answer to their problem. It would help me and relieve them. Only I was never consulted until after the details had been settled. Barton Hill was a dark district with the smelly waters of the canal running through it. The houses were right on the pavement, and there were yards with privies in them joining back to back with the houses in the next street. There were often drunken quarrels in the street and pots and pans went flying. Gas and coal were used and candles upstairs. The bath was a tin one, which hung on the scullery door and doubled as a clothes tub. People were very kind to me and remarked how much I looked like the dead boy.

Before going to Barton Hill I was settled into a new job in a solicitor's office in St Stephen's Street, but the work was dry and boring. I soon learned to operate the switchboard and how to do the letter copying on the press machine. I also had to read through dry legal documents to make sure there were no mistakes in them. My boss was a hearty man who dined and supped well from mid-day until three o'clock while I ate a sandwich in the office or in St Stephen's Churchyard.

One of the solicitor's clients was a man who usually came in dressed unlike anyone else seen in our offices. He wore tweeds or sometimes working clothes and looked like a farmer or market gardener. His approach was unusual to say the least. He asked penetrating and unexpected questions and made the most outlandish observations. He had a nervous blink-cum-wink. My employer seemed to be on the friendliest of terms with him, although the men were two such opposites.

Both were to play a significant part in the events that were rapidly overtaking me. After a while my wages were raised a little, probably less than my boss spent on his lunch for one day, but I never gave it a thought at the time. I had other pressing problems to cope with back at the little house in Barton Hill.

The couple were embarrassing in their attentions to me, especially the wife. She was apprehensive about me riding my bike as her son had recently been killed on one. Like callous youth I didn't see what that had to do with me. Why should I give up my pride and joy? I was not aware, then, of the fact that they were regarding me for adoption. It was not something I ever thought of, or wanted, in fact I was to oppose the idea to the bitter end and would rather have died than submit to it. Gradually it began to dawn on me that something was afoot. All sorts of hints and suggestions were put out, and gradually the idea that I might change my name to theirs was presented. They pointed out that as their name was Willett, it would only involve changing the first two letters of my name. Gradually a battle of wits and emotions was joined. Rows and threats followed. These were interspersed with tearful pleadings about the dead son. To my shame I can't remember his name, though I expect a psychologist could explain why.

I began to find all manner of excuses to stay out as much as possible. They began to check with the Group Leader who had advertised me, who told me that I was ungrateful for all that was being done for me. There were now veiled threats about how I could be made over to them and many other ideas were left in my mind. It was suggested that I should leave the Scouts and that my bike would be taken from me. I was told that I only had so long to make up my mind, though no actual time was stated.

That lunchtime I went along to another solicitor in our office block to ask advice. I had saved five weeks' pocket money as I knew that fees were paid for advice. I didn't go to my own boss as I felt that would somehow be unprofessional. Of course, the first thing he did after advising me was to contact my own boss, as I hadn't said anything about keeping it secret. He refused the fee, which surprised me a lot, but advised me that nobody could force me to change my name, nor could they adopt me without my consent.

That was all I wanted to know. The clouds began to clear and he advised me to confide in my new Sea Scout Captain whom he evidently knew, and probably contacted too. I went to see Skip, as advised, and he assured me he would stand by me and that his mother could give me temporary accommodation. He also gave me change and his telephone number at work in case of need.

There followed a period of intense activity at the office. First my boss called me in and asked me to tell him the whole story, then advised me not to do anything without consulting him first. Then his client with the tweed clothes began paying numerous visits to the office, and whenever he came I was asked to go out and sit in his car 'in case the police wanted to know whose it was'. It was a big MG sports car, but he also had a small MG which I thought strange considering that he was a Socialist. I believed that everyone should have the same share of wealth.

It was evidently necessary to contact my father in London, but before any decisive steps could be taken the crisis was reached. On Friday the Willetts told me that the Group Leader who had sent me to them would be round that evening. I packed my case secretly, changed into my Scout uniform and went down to the river. I think it was nearly the end of October. Skip was there at Scouts and asked me how things were. I told him I might have to leave that night. He was due to be on night work but said that his brother-in-law in Clifton would take a message.

It was dark and misty as I made my way back along the Feeder Canal. Those dark waters seemed to presage happenings as sombre as they were. I reached Aitken Street and put my bike in the passage. I could hear the strident tones of the Group Leader long before entering and was well aware that a storm awaited me. He marched out into the passage and grabbed the bicycle, saying that I was not fit to have anything like that and then there followed a scene in which all sorts of charges were made about me. Here were three adults, one verging on hysteria, and one rather pale fresh faced boy of 15 years of age standing there defying them. The whole affair was very badly handled and so angry did they become that the Group Leader ordered me to take off my uniform as I was no longer fit to be a Scout and that I could do as I pleased as I would soon come running back when I'd had a taste of the world.

I went upstairs, changed out of my uniform, packed it with the rest of my belongings, rejecting anything 'they' had bought me, took my case and hurried downstairs. They wouldn't say goodbye and I slammed the door behind me. As I left the house I could hear the bus coming along Barrow Road, going to the Centre, so I ran and arrived just in time to jump on board. I had enough to pay my fare and telephone my friends. The bus stopped opposite the statue of Neptune and I got off and walked across the Centre. There seemed to be no phone box so I went to the Western Daily Press Offices in Baldwin Street, where I asked if I could pay to use their phone. They gave me permission. I

phoned the Clifton number and was told to wait by
the statue where I would be picked up. Although it
was nearly 11 o'clock at night Skip's relatives came
and took me to their grocery shop in Clifton where
I was given supper and a bed in the flat above the
shop, where the family lived.

The next day my boss sent a telegram to my
father and summoned Skip to a conference with his
client 'Mr Tucker' in his office. It was agreed that I
should stay with Skip's parents for the time being,
and that when my father came it would be decided
what would happen. Someone suggested that it
would be a good idea for Mr Tucker to take me to
his place for lunch, which I think was a device to
introduce me to the Tuckers. Whether Mrs Tucker
was ever consulted about her husband's idea I very
much doubt. She was very kind to me and as
happy a person as you could wish to meet. They
lived in a lovely bungalow south of Bristol near the
airport and did turkey farming and market gar-
dening. It was more of a hobby than a necessity to
Mr Tucker, but he drove himself hard and everyone
else too.

I went back to Skip's mother, who was very kind
and understanding, and in a few days my father
was on the scene. I was now in his care again as the
Group Scout Leader had relinquished all legal
responsibility for me, and now a new proposition
was put to me.

I was asked if I would like to go and live with the
Tucker family. I could stay on at my job and even be
given training in that direction. As things turned
out, Law did not become my chosen career, though

my son has followed that profession. Meanwhile my father was not impressed by the recent events and was thankful that a ready-made solution was at hand. It was up to me, was his comment.

We lunched at the Tuckers again and it was all settled that I should move there. My father returned to London for the second time without his son.

Mr Tucker soon made it known that I was there only to be a productive member of the family. I paid as much as I could towards the cost of my upkeep. It was difficult but I supplemented my pocket money by delivering local letters in my own time. On Saturdays and early mornings before office hours I worked with the turkeys and tomatoes. There were five guard dogs. One was a lovely old English sheep dog called Rough. I thought a lot of Rough, she was a wonderful dog and great pal of mine. She was also a wonderful dog at rounding up sheep, and indeed turkeys for that matter. In fact she became indirectly the reason for my leaving the farm and going to London.

The final point was reached one fine spring Sunday morning. I had let the dogs off to exercise and was trying to press my trousers, much to Mrs Tucker's amusement, when the telephone rang. Her husband answered and it was soon apparent that something was wrong.

'The dogs!' he shouted. 'They're down the road killing the farmer's sheep and he says he'll shoot them if we don't call them off in five minutes.'

I didn't wait to hear more. I was down the road like a streak of lightning. Scenes of Rough being shot were flashing through my mind. I got to the field to find the farmer, gun in hand, pointing at the dogs, two of which were still worrying the sheep trapped in the hedge. There seemed to be blood and wool everywhere. The farmer was scared to touch the biggest Airedale, but I rushed in without thinking and grabbed him by the scruff of the neck. He was head and shoulders into the sheep and we came out covered in blood. Meanwhile Rough was quietly rounding up other sheep as though she was at the trials. I ordered her back. She had not taken part in the savaging. I think the farmer feared I was in danger from these fierce dogs.

The sheep cost quite a bit in compensation money and they marked the end of my stay in that place. My bags were packed and my father summoned. After collecting the wages due to me I said my farewells and was soon on the road to the capital. I would be 16 in a month's time.

My father found me lodgings near Sloane Square and I found myself once again in squalid inner-city conditions. While there I was accepted by John Lewis of Oxford Street working in the silk-sorting department. A few months later, having given in my notice there over a question of promotion, I applied to Sainsbury's, where I was given thorough training in the grocery trade.

I was very short of money while at Sainsbury's. The wage was low and I had to clothe myself. My father sent me the occasional small gift, otherwise I don't know how I could have managed. It drove me to stealing from the shop. The method I will not divulge, as others may be tempted to copy it. Years later, after my conversion, I wrote to the firm confessing my deeds and sent them a token cheque which they accepted, and forgave my acts without further recourse. The manager was very suspicious of me and tried to catch me. He did once but I boldly put the money at his feet and he didn't notice it. How? Well, as I've said – I won't tell you.

Following these adventures I had a number of jobs, too numerous to mention them all, and as many adventures to match them. They took me from Bristol to London, from there to Bognor Regis and back to London.

At one stage I shared one room with my father until after the blitzes in 1940. We lived right in the thick of the bombed area where I was hard worked by day and terrified by night, as were most of us living in the London area. I returned to Bristol in 1941 just in time for the blitzes on this city. By the time I joined the Merchant Navy I had worked in an estate agent's office, solicitor's office, three grocers' shops, a machine tool company's office, a radio shop, a hotel, a vet's surgery and an asphalt company's office. I had lived in accommodation with 12 different families.

A Single to Bristol, Please

Following a disagreement with my father I took exactly the amount of pocket money that was due to me for that week and boarded a bus for Bristol. I had nowhere to go that night, so resorted to sleeping rough. Next evening a policeman stopped to speak to me on the Centre.

'Where are you going, sonny?'

'To sleep in an air-raid shelter by the Cenotaph, sir.'

'Oh, and how old are you?'

'Seventeen sir, last April.'

'Where have you come from?'

'London sir, where I was bombed out.'

'Have you any family here?'

'No sir, I was brought up in Bristol from when I was ten.'

'And where was that?' he asked kindly.

'In the Müller Homes on Ashley Down. My father and sisters live in London, but they have nowhere to keep me.'

As it was a warm summer evening, and there was nothing special happening, the kindly cop continued to chat with this very young-looking boy. He'd always wanted to know about these orphans and this lad seemed harmless, well spoken, clean and tidy. But why was he here at 10 o'clock at night?

'So what do you want to do back here in Bristol?' he continued.

'I've got a job in Bridge Street, at the electrical shop, and I start there on Monday.'

'Have you got any money?'

'Yes sir, a shilling and sixpence.'

It would cost me a shilling to get my suitcase from the Tramway Centre, so I had a penny a day to exist on.

'So you're sleeping out till you start this job?'

'Yes sir.'

'Good luck then, look after yourself and keep out of mischief.'

'Thank you sir, I will.'

The pennies were used sparingly. A bag of stale buns and cakes were bought daily from the Bakers. Then a wash and brush-up in the gents, with water to drink, and back to the air-raid shelter at night. One incident is worth recording. There were two other occupants of the shelter.

The man stirred as I entered. 'Keep away from her, she's lousy!' he whispered, pointing to a bundle sleeping in the far corner.

I had no intention of getting anywhere near the woman. This advice had been given by a man I shall never forget. His accent was Cockney. He told me his story that night.

He had married a London Flower Girl from Oxford Circus. She was only 17 and died in childbirth in their first year of marriage. He went into a drunken stupor which lasted about 17 years. One day he met a man in a down-and-out's shelter who told him about the love of God and how God gave His Son to die for us.

'From that time my life changed,' he said.

'And now for the past 20 years I have worked among down-and-outs. Each summer I do casual work for farmers and spend my money on those in need, and to keep myself moving around so I can share God's love with them.'

At 18 I was deeply moved by this missionary to the down-and-outs. If ever I became a Christian I would like to be real like my friend. We met once again, about seven years later. He was working on a farm near Bristol and was on his rounds. I was able to tell him that I was now a follower of Jesus and was visiting some of the people who had helped me since leaving the orphanage. In my own way I still try to keep in touch with a variety of people, as he did.

Monday came, and with it my new job. The manager told me he and his wife were living in the Worcester Hotel in Clifton, and asked if I would like a room there until I found a place to live. I could have it free if I helped in the hotel. It seemed simple, and almost solved the problem, but not quite, as events turned out.

During the first week at the shop, the manager told me he would be leaving at the end of the week and wanted me to leave also and help run the hotel. 'In fact you would not be able to stay at the shop as the owners are returning to take over,' he said.

Mr and Mrs Lewis spent time talking to me and were delighted to find that I had been trained by Sainsbury's, London food shops, and that I had been four years in a Bristol orphanage where the children did most of the domestic chores – even the boys. Well! Well! They could hardly believe their luck. I seemed tailor-made for their new venture.

The guests took to me. The solicitor promised me his shoes when he went into the army. The old ladies twittered over me and the young blonde from the Ministry asked me to help her by holding the hair-dryer! I took meals in to Lady Percy next door who asked a lot of questions. She knew the owners of the hotel and her brother was a Director of the BBC in Whiteladies Road. Maybe I would like a job there?

This wonderful state of affairs soon came to a dramatic end. The Lewises went out for a day's shopping, returning for meals and leaving the running of the place to me. After evening drinks one day they went out and never came back.

The hotel ran on much as usual for the morning, but when people came looking for the Lewises, it was obvious that they had disappeared in a hurry. Lady Percy was brilliant. She contacted the owners and took over the running of the hotel until they came. The car, the goods and all available cash had gone.

Lady Percy had arranged an interview for me at the BBC, but the night before, the studio was set on fire by a lad around my age with a German father and British mother. He was in the Hitler Youth Movement and spoke perfect English and German and as you may guess, my interview was cancelled due to the suspicion aroused by our similar backgrounds.

I now had to find somewhere to work as well as somewhere to live and soon found temporary work in a vet's surgery in Berkeley Square.

'Don't go near the black cat in the cage on its own, Collett' said the vet. 'It's been in an air raid and was sitting on its owner's lap when a bomb made a direct hit and killed the old lady.'

'John will be away so he'll give you all the instructions about what the job means.'

John showed me around and he too emphasised the care I should take with the black cat. It crouched in the back of its cage and hissed at any approach. To touch its cage sent it flying round the walls in a blind panic. It was a ball of fur with blazing eyes and claws and teeth bared.

I would listen to the advice and follow it to the letter!

'You come on at 6 this evening and finish at 6 in the morning. On Saturday evening you're free until Sunday.'

The pay was quite good – about £2 a week, payable on Friday morning.

John went off to Somerset, a very nice guy who did all he could to help me. The vet and his secretary looked in during the evening and seemed pleased. They didn't stay long but left a telephone number 'only to be used in an emergency. Always ask for the vet.'

I felt a lot of sympathy for the black cat and always chatted to it as I passed its cage. I also gave it a little whistle like a bird song when I was nearby.

My boss was pleased after the first week's work and put a little extra on to my pay. 'How are you getting on Collett?'

'Fine sir, and I'm getting to know the black cat too.'

'Good for you son, you might tame him soon. He needs a lot of attention but unless we can find someone who can understand him and handle him he'll have to go.'

'I hope to be friendly with him soon and then perhaps I can persuade my landlady to let me keep him.'

'Good luck if you can, and I'll be happy to let you have him.'

Everything went along well during the next two weeks. We had a few more air raids both at night and during the day.

Gradually 'Black Bomber', as I now called him, and I got to know each other better. One night he came to the front of his cage as I came on duty, and when I called and whistled to him, he purred and rubbed himself against the bars. The orphan boy and the orphaned cat had struck up a friendship.

For the first time I was able to stroke him. A few nights later I took him carefully out of his cage while I was having my break. He shared my supper and then climbed up on my lap. Fear had been conquered by loving care and lots of contact.

Next day I told my boss what had happened. 'That's very good Collett. I'm glad you've succeeded in helping "Black Bomber". Good name for him too. But I've heard from John today and he wants to re-start this Saturday, a week earlier than expected, so I'll pay you off and you can take Bomber with you if your landlady agrees.'

'She does Sir, and I'll be sorry to go. I've enjoyed working here but it will be nice to be in a day-time job again.'

'Have you got one yet?'

'No Sir, but I'm due for an interview next week. Can I have a reference please?'

John came back and I got full pay for the four weeks and took Bomber home with me. That night there was an air raid. I had already found myself another job as firewatcher in Clifton. A drunken Irish man lurched toward me and handed me an unexploded firebomb he'd picked up on the way through. I promptly put it into a bucket of sand. The whole of Bristol seemed to be ablaze. I was in Clifton, so not in the main target area.

The nearest bomb that night made a direct hit between the vet's and the adjoining YWCA in Berkeley Square. John and all the animals were killed: the vet and his assistant were operating and both severely injured. There was terrible loss of life as over 30 young women were killed and others injured.

As I went into the square after the bombing stopped there was a scene of chaos, ARP, fire brigade, police, ambulances, etc. I met a friend who stared at me in disbelief. 'I thought you were dead! I've just told the police you were working in the vet's kennels when the bomb went off. What happened?'

'John came back a week early and so here I am still alive!'

Since then I feel I've been living on 'borrowed' time.

Where next? I wanted to avoid joining the armed forces in case I killed my cousins who might be fighting for the other side. I figured out that the supply of food and essential oil and petrol would help to save life rather than destroy it, so my next decision was to go along to the Merchant Navy Shipping Office, which started me on another set of adventures.

'God Sends the Food, but...'

My career in catering had started seriously in Bristol. To be precise in the Worcester Hotel, Clifton. Like all boys I've had a healthy interest in food. In all the places I've lived I had to do basic housework and room tidying. Landladies insisted on it, as did the children's homes. My six months at 'The Worcester', two years at Sainsbury's and five years at sea were all part of that process.

I joined my first ship at Avonmouth Dock in August 1941. I was signed on as a mess room boy but never actually did that job as another boy joined at the same time, as cabin boy, and our jobs were swapped. There was no rivalry between us, and we were the best of friends; it was all decided on the first day aboard when we had to wash up all used dishes in the captain's pantry. I don't think there were any dishes left that had not been used!

I was familiar with nautical terms as a result of my Sea Scout days and was handy about the ship. I was never seasick. When the boat left port I would feel drowsy and would go for a 'watch below' or 'pillow-drill' as we called a siesta. On awakening some 20 minutes later I had a head as clear as a bell and had found my 'sea legs'. No matter what the weather from now on I was totally at home and felt at one with the ship. Only if we had a bad helmsman on the bridge during a rough night would I be disturbed. Then a feeling of unease would awaken me to make me listen to the wind shrieking through the rigging and the screws racing as they came out of the water under our cabin, causing the ship to shudder from stem to stern. The constant juddering and 'pop-popping' of the steering-gear motors on the other side of our cabin did not disturb us after the first night at sea.

We often had disturbed nights, though, as the alarm bells called us to action stations. Many a night we tumbled into our 'siren' suits of rubber and put on sea-boots and Wellington capes to go up to the top-bridge called the 'Monkey Island'. Here we would peer through the filthy weather, looking for enemy aircraft, submarines and mines. On a fine night it wasn't too bad, but then the enemy did not often choose fine nights for their murderous attacks. I was perched out on the wing of the Monkey Island very often, but scarcely saw anything worthwhile. We were glad when the all clear went and we could return to our bunks to get as much sleep as possible before 6 a.m. Later I was moved from lookout, when it was discovered that I was very short-sighted.

I was put instead on the telephone aft to relay orders from the bridge to the gun crews on the anti-aircraft, and to submarine guns on the stern. I was also a Lewis machine gunner, but only succeeded in shooting down in flames an anti-divebomber balloon in St George's Channel.

Another time I wondered why our AA gun's crew had ceased firing although planes were still attacking us. I found it was because I was firing tracer bullets across them, having failed to put the 'stop' on my swivelling stand. They were, of course, hiding from the hail of shots coming from the deck below, but fortunately I ran out of ammo at that point, and was promoted to communications thereafter. I had a good clear voice and this proved more useful than my prowess as a gunner.

After my second trip I had a good discharge and was sent on leave. I could now sign on as an Assistant Steward, and this gave me some extra pay and a uniform of patrol jackets.

So my first two years at sea were as a cabin boy, assistant steward and then full steward. I chose not to go further up the stewarding ladder, that is, cleaning cabins, waiting at tables and other housekeeping chores. I rejected the idea of becoming a radio operator as they were shut into a stuffy radio room with no portholes. They did have uniforms but were not given much status. They had to work 12 hours on duty and then 12 hours off.

I started as an assistant cook and baker after six weeks at the Cardiff Sea School. I'd had the benefit of two years at Sainsbury's in London, Bognor Regis and Hoxton in the East End. (I remember they practised magic in Hoxton and on one occasion a whole crate of eggs and a side of bacon was 'spirited away' between the lorry and the shop. It was dark and we all had blackout curtains but the Assistant Manager was supervising! We had Buckingham Palace as one of our customers. I only went into the Palace once – to help deliver some hors d'oeuvres for a banquet.)

After two years in the Stewarding Department and my time at the Cardiff Sea School I became a ship's cook and had a cabin to myself furnished with carpets, fan and heater.

My first job in that capacity was during the Normandy Invasion. I joined as second cook and baker at the East India Dock during the flying bomb raids on London.

The cook and I were both newly signed-on, but he was excitable and unpredictable, especially when drinking, which he did more than I first realised. After a few culinary disasters the crew refused to sail unless the cook was sacked.

The Skipper loved his curry for breakfast every day and until he discovered that I – the second cook and baker – was responsible for them, he tried to hold on to him, but the crew got up a round-robin demand and he was dismissed.

I was promoted and a new second cook signed on. I did not want this sudden early promotion because I knew that I needed to learn a lot more to become really efficient. 'Sorry Mate, but there's a war on' was the cry. So I became a Chief Petty Officer (in RN terms) with a cabin to myself. The ship was a 'Liberty' boat built to British design in New York.

Late one night I had just come aboard and gone to my cabin when I heard a scuffle and some angry shouting in the alleyway leading to my quarters. We were loading petrol and oil aboard the modern oil tanker I had sailed in for about six months. My second cook was a Welshman. I had signed aboard the ship while it was in Swansea Bay since the ship's cook had signed off sick and the ship was waiting to sail. There were a number of local seamen on board, some of whom spoke Welsh. I had picked up a few phrases from my Father and a Welshman who kept a paper shop in Blackfriars Road.

Now he was coming along with a jerrycan of petrol proclaiming what he was going to do to me – in Welsh, and to the whole world. His drinking pals knew the danger of what he was trying to do.

Here we were loading up with hundreds of tons of petrol which, if he had set fire to me, and to my cabin, would have sent the whole ship – if not the whole terminal, up in flames. All of us were in equal danger, and that night we had a breathtaking escape. I once saw an advert, which read 'Beer is best'. Some wag had inserted 'left alone!!'

A ship's cook is not a glamorous job as the second part of the title suggests when it says 'but the devil sends the cooks.'

Food and essential materials such as clothes, shoes, furniture, etc., were rationed for about eight years during and after the Second World War. Everyone was entitled to coupons for food, clothes and furniture. These were issued in ration books. Petrol also was another scarce commodity and of course there was a 'black market' in all these goods. One skipper of a ship I sailed in was reputed to have 40 drums of 50 gallons each of petrol, which were shipped ashore before the cargo was discharged. I was able to fill up my petrol tank on at least one occasion. Petrol was then about 15 pence at the pumps but 56 pence on the black market.

On trips back home I usually took a suitcase of scarce foods, toys, dolls and cosmetics. On one trip I took a full set of china from Maceys 5th Ave. for my landlady Mrs Dillon. I nursed it in my bunk during some terrible storms in the North Atlantic, but when it reached Temple Meads Station, Bristol, a porter ran his barrow into it and broke a few pieces. He did what Hitler and the storms failed to do. I never remember paying customs on them, although I did usually declare them.

I think the customs turned a blind eye, thinking that we deserved a 'perk' if anyone did, as so many merchant seamen lost their lives or were injured.

Most ships were victualled – stocked up with food – abroad if that were possible. With refrigerators, large cans and dried fruit that was generally possible. We took fresh food aboard whenever that was available. On one occasion we re-stocked a hospital ship in the Mediterranean. We had to do without potatoes for about six months.

The first ship I sailed on as cook was the *Samakron*. All those hundreds of ships were pre-fabricated, some built in less than two weeks, and most of them had 'Sam...' as their prefix. Presumably for 'Uncle Sam' i.e. the USA. Others had the prefix 'Empire' and I was on one of them when I decided to sign off a few years later. By then I was heartily sick of the sea, and of my job as a cook. I never did get that essential extra training as a chef, although I still help my wife with the family cooking!

On the way to the Normandy Invasion I was cook on an ammunition ship to supply Allied troops landing at Arromanches. Along with all the high explosives we carried NAAFI stores – including what the crew called 'Hooch' – alcoholic drink. We had left the East India Docks and were at anchor off Southend pier and were having problems with a number of the crew being drunk, although not allowed ashore. The nights were dark but there was the constant drone 'URR URR' of the V1 'doodle-bugs' sounding like giant motor bikes overhead.

Hearing running feet outside my cabin I went out on deck. It was a warm summer evening. The second mate was standing at the rail overlooking the cargo hatches. He shone a torch onto the far end of the hatch, which had been forced open, and was ordering some crew members to come up onto the deck, when the crack of a gun and a flash from it was followed by the whine of a bullet fired at us. That set the alarm bells ringing, and us scurrying for cover. The police were radioed and soon their boat drew alongside. A number of the crew were taken ashore and their war effort ended in Wormwood Scrubs. When we set sail for the channel there was a long trail of empty bottles that followed us down to the Mulberry Harbour off Caen in Normandy.

One last danger faced me on that passage. Not only the shelling of German long-range guns from 30 miles inland, but the shorter-range axe of a drunken crew member who came looking for me. The axe was of American make – because being on a Liberty boat built in USA it differed from English ones in that it was all steel, including the handle, and had a steel hook at the back of the axehead. This saved my life. When this shouting madman came looking for me – by name – he crashed into our cabin, which I shared with two others, and swung the axe behind him, aiming at the top bunk where I had been asleep.

The hook caught the stanchion behind him as he tried to swing the axe up to reach me. It held him back long enough for me to leap out of the bunk and out through the cabin door, which banged shut behind me, saving me from the blow which embedded the axe head into it. This shipmate was fined for taking the axe out of its case in the alleyway and so endangering the whole crew. I spent a sleepless night on a settee in one of the mess rooms. That was one of the most terrifying nights of my life.

George at sea with his mates (front row, middle)

Meat Boat to Buenos Aires

'It's a good job you got your signals right this time, skipper, or we'd have blasted you to Kingdom come!' said the booming voice coming out of the darkness of the South Atlantic night.

There had been the Battle of the River Plate and defeat of the German 'pocket' battleship *Graf Spee*. I was on the Glasgow-registered *Moveria* sailing across to New York in convoy. The weather had been so bad that the convoy was scattered over the Western Approaches and had become completely unmanageable, so we had the signal to make our own way unescorted to our various destinations. Our ship headed South for Buenos Aires to load up with meat, etc. We were a large refrigerated cargo-passenger liner mostly crewed by Scotsmen.

'The best feeding ships in the Merchant Navy,' my Scots friend told me. He came from Kirkintilloch, 'the place where a dozen Scotsmen were injured when a taxi crashed', he said with a twinkle in his eye. The feeding part was in fact quite true, as we fed like lords even though there was rationing ashore in Europe.

During the days of the storm we lost two of our four lifeboats and had one of the remaining two also damaged. (When we eventually reached port, both of these filled with water and sank. So we were actually relying on a few life rafts for survival, unbeknown to us then.) We had heard that there might be other German battleships in the South Atlantic. This was in 1942. We sailed on into warmer, calmer weather and had begun to enjoy a much more pleasant trip until about midnight about two to three days away from our destination.

Out of the pitch darkness on our starboard beam (right side) came two blinding searchlights and a cultured voice that commanded us to 'heave-to or we'll blast you out of the water'. Our skipper had come out of retirement as a farmer, because of the great loss of Merchant Seamen caused by the war at sea. He looked like a farmer much more than a skipper. In this frightening situation someone up on the Bridge had got it wrong. The recognition signal-flags did not tally. The searchlights dipped off and on a few times and we could hear the engines of a very large vessel, the bells and sounds of it as it manoeuvred, possibly to blast us out of the water. I was standing near the lifeboat with a life jacket on among my shipmates, preparing to take to the boats and shivering despite the warm tropical night.

One of my mates who shared our cabin was already in the lifeboat. He often slept in it – and although a big, strong fellow his nerve had completely gone and he was invalided out after this trip. I felt very sorry for him.

There was a lot of scurrying about on the bridge

as the flags were changed, and one turned up the wrong way. 'Hang up your "dohbi" (washing), skipper,' someone shouted from among the crew aft. We got it right on the final time. It seemed like an eternity as we waited in the warm southern air for what might be our last moments. Then we heard the crackling of the British battleship's public address system as she steamed up alongside us and gave our skipper 'a right old rollicking' as one chap expressed it. Soon we continued on our way to the Rio de la Plata – River Plate – to Buenos Aires, Berisso and La Plata to take on board our cargo of meat, butter, etc.

We were also refitted with four new steel lifeboats powered by engines to replace the wooden ones, which had to be dredged up from the harbour when lowered into the water – they leaked like sieves!

On the way home a month later we became Commodore ship of a small, fast convoy and tried out two of our new lifeboats in the anchorage off Freetown, West Africa. I was in the first one, which was supposed to be away for an hour. The second one followed after our engine failed and they had an engineer aboard to help us back to the ship at anchor. Their engine also failed, and by now the tide was so strong that we were carried up river and had to row hard in an extremely heavy boat to tie up by the shore. It was 12 hours before the tide turned and we made it back to the ship just after midnight, very tired, hungry and sunburnt. We had only had hard-tack biscuits and water to drink. We had an almost uneventful trip home to 'Dear Auld Glasgie Toon', except that a German U-boat (submarine) was sunk by our escorts and some RAF planes, as it lay in wait for us off our port (left) bow. Two destroyers stayed after dropping depth charges and ramming the submarine when she surfaced. They brought along some of the wreckage and a German sailor's hat with the name and number of the U-boat on the hatband.

I too was half German through my mother, the reason I refused to join the armed forces and be trained to kill, choosing instead one of the most dangerous jobs of the war, so although I was glad I had escaped being torpedoed I did feel sorry for those other young seamen who had perished in a watery grave. I was certainly not ready to die at that time.

During more than five years at sea I had never met a man who actually told me that he was a practising Christian, except for one man who visited the ship while in dock, preparing to sail. He came aboard in Bristol one warm, sunny afternoon. Most of the crew were asleep after their night out and the Sunday morning 'liveners' before a big roast dinner. This visitor was an old man about 75 or 80 years old. I was preparing the fish and chips for supper when he appeared, struggling up the gangway puffing and blowing.

Were any of the crew about, did I think? I told him that the crew were resting in their cabins and that they wouldn't be 'about' until about 5 o'clock. Was there anything I could do to help? He explained that he had some books that he wanted to give them. I knew that they wouldn't welcome being disturbed at this time and would probably treat him roughly and throw his books away.

'Look, Pop,' I said, 'I'll give them the books when they come up to get their supper. I'll make sure that they all get one.' He said that was very kind of me and gave me enough for all the officers and crew. Then he went rather wearily down the gangway after I'd given him a cup of tea and a sit down in the galley.

I picked up the pile of books and found that they were Christian literature. After leafing through the booklets I put them into bundles for each of the different departments but made sure that none were left for me. When asked why I didn't have one I told them that I already knew all about the Bible and religion because I had that rammed down my throat for 14 years: 'Three times a day and five times on Sunday.'

Some five or six years later I went aboard a similar ship with another man who distributed Christian literature on a Sunday afternoon. He insisted on going into the cabins and waking men up to 'give them the Gospel'. He got a predictable reception and most of his books were torn up and left floating in the harbour. When I suggested that he had chosen a difficult time of day I was put firmly in my place. That was my only experience as a Christian going aboard the ships in Bristol docks.

There is a time when the fish bite, as every good fisherman knows, and although they may use a lot of bait at other times, they seldom make good catches.

Sealed Orders

Setting out from Avonmouth aboard the *Athelchief* we were heading for Belfast Lough. I was part of the crew of an oil tanker bound for New York hoping to be home by Christmas. She was a beautiful ship. Quite new, not like some of the 'old crocks' I'd sailed in earlier. She was built originally for the Norwegians and many notices were in that language. Sure enough, we crossed the Atlantic to New York and anchored off Ellis Island – hoping to take on board our cargo of petrol and oil.

'They're taking a long time to get us started,' my friend the carpenter remarked.

'Perhaps they've run dry now that the Yanks have entered the war! Pearl Harbor was a terrible shock.'

'So now we're fighting the Japanese as well as the Germans and the Italians.'

'Yep!' he said. 'But we do have the Americans on our side, and that evens things up for the Allied Forces.'

Still we were swinging around on our anchor chain, going with the tide. At last we got up steam and the Pilot came aboard – but not to dock in New Jersey, only to get us back out to sea! We were sailing under sealed orders and not in convoy –

dangerous assignment, this! Soon we headed south
and the rumours buzzed. Finally, after riding out a
hurricane in the Gulf of Mexico for two days, we
docked in Houston, Texas. Here we loaded up with
one of the first '100 octane' cargoes produced, suitable for modern planes and tanks, then on to
Galveston, Port Arthur and Beaumont and on to
Cuba. There we awaited orders, fully expecting to
be home for Christmas. All this changed as our next
orders were to head south and through the Panama
Canal which took us out to the Pacific Ocean.
'Where now?' we wondered. We were heading
south to Cape Horn under sealed orders with no
idea of our final destination.

The distance to Cape Horn is over 4000 miles and
there was not much to see during those weeks of
travelling. We did see some interesting marine life,
mostly birds and fish, the most notable of which
was the albatross. They are said never to come
north of the Equator. We picked up a contingent of
these very large birds one bright, clear night. The
moon had not yet risen and the air was warm, so we
sat on the after-deck chatting, with someone playing a mouth organ in the background. Suddenly we
became conscious of a mewing noise as though
there were a kitten about. Rather mystified, we
began to wonder if a cat had stowed away in
Panama and had produced kittens.

While puzzling over this I detected a shadow in
the sky above us, and there we discovered a very
large bird hovering almost noiselessly above us.
Then we found others and they were 'mewing'
softly to each other. During the remainder of that

voyage and until we docked in Capetown, one at
least of these birds was with us all the way.

There were huge seas, with 20–40 ft waves, and
cold but beautiful weather. Tierra del Fuego – Land
of Fire – was an apt name for Cape Horn when seen
with the sun shining on its icy peaks. Here we
steered east, passing south of the Falkland Islands
where they said an old Bristol ship, the SS *Great
Britain*, had lain a wreck for many years. We were
now with nothing between us and the South Polar
regions, and had been sailing for 7–8 weeks when
we received fresh instructions by radio to continue
east to South Africa.

Coming round the Horn, we had a following
wind and sea. It was a most exhilarating experience, unless you suffered from seasickness. The
ship was pushed up from the stern as though by a
giant hand and the waves alongside would tower
up. There we would hang momentarily as a child at
the top of a slide. Then with a hissing and gurgling
we would slide down to the troughs below us. Now
the sea was towering ahead and we would then
receive another tremendous thrust up to the crest of
the wave following and go hissing again into the
trough below. The ship was tilted as steeply as
Porlock Hill and sometimes almost seemed as
though it must go stern over bow in a giant cart-
wheel manoeuvre. I expect any ship going in the
reverse direction against the elements found it to be
frustrating in the extreme.

Once on our way across the South Atlantic we
saw one of the miracles of oceanic migration. For
about 36 hours we heard and saw a vast cavalcade

of very large fish travelling on a similar course to ours but about three miles off on our starboard bow. We heard them before we saw them, as they came up in the gloaming of the Antarctic night and began over-hauling us. The sea seemed to bubble and boil as they made their way like crowds of children coming out of school to go on their summer holidays. They were whistling, squealing, grunting and producing just about every human and animal noise it seemed possible to make. The Mate lent me his binoculars to take a closer look.

He said he had never seen anything like it, though he had heard that these migrations happened every so many years. The bosun had seen them before, while on whaling ships in the Antarctic Ocean off Australia and New Zealand, but then he was the only man among us who had ever been round the Horn before, or had sailed on a sailing ship. He was then over 70, we reckoned, as strong as an ox and about 6 ft 7 in tall.

As we neared Capetown the weather warmed up. Still our faithful albatrosses were with us. It was now a very long time since we had been ashore in Texas. Also we had received no mail. We were sure that we had become a ghost ship and were like the Ancient Mariner of S.T. Coleridge's poem. We could see the beautiful harbour of Capetown, but the seas were so rough that we had orders to steam outside for a further day and a half. The Cape Rollers were said to have capsized a few ships and they wouldn't risk us losing such a valuable cargo of Aviation Spirit that we had on board. When we finally got in and were docked it was to be for only 24 hours.

From the Cape we headed North to Aden, one of the hottest spots in the world, through the Red Sea and the Suez Canal and thence to Alexandria on the Mediterranean.

The Mountain that Smoked

As a cabin boy and steward I got to learn a lot of things that I could never have learned had I been a deck hand or in the engine room. Maybe if I had been a wireless operator I would have learned more. That was a boring job shut up in a hot stuffy cabin for 12 hours at a stretch. Many ships did not carry them before the war. Now there were at least two of them. They were called 'sparks' – 'neither fowl, fish nor fine red herring' was how they were described by the Navigating Officer.

I took him his mug of tea in the chart room.

'You know, steward, that we're going to pass the place where Moses received the Ten Commandments tomorrow morning?'

'Yes Sir. It was at Sinai, wasn't it?'

'Smart lad. Where did you learn that?'

'At my schools in London and in Bristol.'

'That's Avonmouth the seaport, isn't it?'

'Yes sir, but there are also boats sailing from the city centre.'

'Have you been in the Suez Canal before?'

'No sir, but I would like to see the mountain.'

'You'll have to be up by 4.00 a.m. lad.'

'I will sir. Where will it be?'

'Over on our starboard (right) as we head up the Red Sea. It is over 7000 feet high.'

'How near will it be sir?'

'It will be 120 miles inland, but with the sun shining on it, and the rest of us in darkness, on a clear day it seems much closer.'

I had a world atlas in my cabin, so I went down and looked it up. There it was just as the Chief Mate said. I've never had a problem getting up early, so there I was up on deck at 4.00 a.m. Sure enough the top of Sinai was standing out from the mists with the searchlight of the sun picking it out. A shiver ran down my spine as all sorts of memories, images and pictures from the illustrated Bible crowded through my mind. I could see the old man with a flowing beard and long white hair gazing up into the brightness above and around him. In his arms were the two stone tablets. The Ten Commandments. It was one of the most memorable moments of my 20 short years. I went down to the cabin where my shipmates lay asleep and found that I was shivering.

Time seemed to stand still, I found it was nearly time to get up, so went off for a shower and to the galley to get my mates up with a mug of tea.

'Come off it Collett. You don't believe all that stuff they teach in Sunday Schools?'

'Yes, I do. I've actually seen the place mentioned in the Bible where God gave Moses the Ten Commandments.'

'You're not religious are you? Because you tell risqué jokes – more than most of us.'

'Just believing it doesn't make you a Christian.'

'Well what does?'

'Er, well... practising it, I suppose.' Loud guffaws and touching of heads followed. But it is true, isn't it?

As I was on an oil tanker, we passed up and down the Suez Canal a few times on our way to Abadan in the Persian Gulf. We went to Italy, India and Australia. My final journey was meant to take us to Japan. I never forgot Moses on the Mountain, but got used to passing through the canal without much comment. We often had debates about religion, but I was always careful to point out that I was not one of them. There was nothing wrong with my head! The problem was in my will.

We were heading for 'Special Operations in the Far East'. This was the first trip in over five years when I sold up everything and said goodbye to my friends in Bristol. I made every preparation for what I expected would be my last trip. 'Except for preparing to meet God!' We often heard services on the Overseas Service of the BBC, and I was deeply moved by such old hymns as 'Nearer my God to Thee' and 'For those in peril on the seas'.

At 6.00 a.m. we were sailing along the oily waters of the Suez Canal, and there alongside was the desert patrol riding their camels as they patrolled the sides of the canal. We were a ship sailing through the desert. They were on the 'ships of the desert'. It was all rather romantic, but I wouldn't say that to the bunch of men who were my shipmates. They never seemed to believe anything. Just hooted and jeered at anything serious.

The Suez Canal was a very different proposition from the Panama. It was a channel through the desert.

There were various lay-bys as the Canal was not wide enough for ships to pass. There were also various lakes where ships were at anchor awaiting their turn to proceed, but we were given priority as we had a dangerous cargo. The Captain had to hand his ship over to the Canal Pilot and his own small crew of boatmen. They did all the exterior work of tying up the ship from their motor boat. A large searchlight was fitted up to the bow of the ship and so we were on our way along the 100 miles or so to the Mediterranean Sea end. Part of the journey was by night, and this is when I had the rather unusual view of the camel patrol not very far from my porthole. We did have a swim whilst the ship was at anchor in the lakes, but the water was so warm that we didn't stay in for long. I went in about midnight but was glad to come out and have a shower to clean off the canal residue before turning in. There were large areas of phosphorescence in the water so that when diving and swimming the body was encased in a silvery sheen. We saw a lot more of these when crossing the Indian Ocean later on in the voyage. We had a great time bargaining with the bum-boats off Port Said, and here we learned that we were to discharge at Alexandria, also in Egypt.

Alexandria, named after Alexander the Great, was a huge sprawling city. Out in the bay lay the ruins of Paphos lighthouse, built about 300 BC, and once 440 ft high, but now a pile of huge fallen stones. This was the first time in Egypt for most of us. We had only been allowed ashore while loading in Texas for about one week and refuelling in Capetown for one day. Quite a number of our crew had been 'mugged' in Capetown and one was left behind in hospital, being found seriously wounded on the slopes of Table Mountain. These happenings served to warn us of the dangers of the dockside area at night and were added to by further warnings from our more experienced shipmates. Soon now we would be aboard the clanking trams, in taxis or gharries heading for Mohamed Ali Square.

Ashore in Alexandria – Attemped Murders

'Going ashore' are two magic words to the sailor. Getting trousers and shirts ironed and all our shore gear ready were exciting preparations for the time when we'd be down that gangway and into town. Most docks are away from cities, and transport to and from could be a problem. Taxis, buses and trams, and sometimes a subway, had to be organised.

Cooks and catering staff have to work most of the time the ship is in port. Seamen expect grub to be available and unless relief staff were supplied, it was our job to be on duty, but tonight I was free and down the gangway we went.

Old clanking trams passed the dock gates on their way to Mohammed Ali Square and we boarded one. It was a warm evening, the air scented with mimosa and frangipani; also, less pleasantly, with the smell of gutters, horse and camel manure. Crowds thronged the wide roads and bustled in and out of narrow side streets. A cacophony of sounds hit our ears – jangling tram bells, honking car horns and shouting of gharry drivers as they whipped their horses along. Stately camels picked their way disdainfully through the streets.

Intermingled with all this were the military vehicles of the Allied Forces, Jeeps, trucks and motorbikes, camouflaged and adding to the din. Robes and fezzes mingled with uniforms and Western-style clothes. Beggars were everywhere calling 'backsheesh' and 'look mister no milk for baby', holding the child with one hand on hip and an empty breast in the other. What confusion! The tram moved on towards the Square, which was a seething mass of people, paradise for pickpockets and thieves. Having been at sea now for about 2½ years, I was aware of this and had my piastres safely stowed away next to my skin.

When we reached the Square we made for the United Services Club. Inside it was hot and noisy with a band and Egyptian dancers on stage. At the back of the main hall was a long bar and in between were tables and chairs filled with servicemen from the Allied countries.

My friends and I got some food and drink and sat at a table at the back. It was smoky and buzzing with conversation in different languages and accents. We were a very small number in 'civvies' but had our MN badges, issued by the Merchant Navy.

My visit to the club ended rather suddenly as I was separated from my shipmates by a fight amongst the Allies, mainly along racial lines, but all of them white!

By the time I got to the tram station the last tram had just left. A naval Petty Officer stood nearby.

'Do you carry a gun?' he asked.

'No I'm afraid not,' was my reply.

'Well, what about a knife?' continued this short, tough sailor. 'I've got both and I used my pistol to shoot my way out of a house last night. They made way for me pretty quickly.' He was older than I and certainly looked a tough character. 'I'm not waiting here any longer,' he said. 'The last tram has probably gone, so I'll go and look for my mates. You can catch it as it passes the end of Sister Street next turning left, if you're quick enough,' he added, looking rather doubtfully at me. He seemed to think I was too soft to risk it.

I might not have weapons, but I was sober, quick to think and act and could run. Fear can speed you up more than drugs, even alcohol, which slows you down as the amount increases. Having made up my mind, I wasted no time in spite of the danger. This was the Red Light district. I could hear the tram clanking along in the distance as I turned down Sister Street and found myself in a very dark place. Shadowy figures were passing to and fro, children coming out of houses offering to introduce their sisters. Here and there were pools of light, a door opened and a woman shouted with a Scottish accent!

I hurried along, keeping away from the houses and was conscious of noises before and behind me, the sound of shuffling sandals and swishing clothes. Signals were being sent ahead. I realised then that I'd walked into a trap and that the warnings I'd been given were real. As I quickened my pace, so they did too. I broke into a run and rushed headlong towards another sound – the clanging of the tram bell ahead. It was now so close, my momentum carried me right out into the light of the main street at the end, and as the tram slowed I jumped onto the already overcrowded rear platform. Looking back I saw my white-robed pursuers standing panting at the end of the dark tunnel.

This was the story I told my mates as we gathered in the Galley for a fry-up of steak and eggs and bacon – those of us who were still sober. Their reaction? 'More fool you for doing such a stupid thing – you were lucky to get away with it. Plenty of others didn't and were fished out of the harbour after being robbed of everything and knifed.'

That was a thought! I was thankful I'd stayed sober that night. Only very rarely did I ever drink more than a shandy while on shore leave. This certainly saved me twice during our stay in Egypt. Looking back I can see that God was looking after me during some hair-raising experiences on land and at sea.

After the previous night's scare I decided to go back to the ship by gharry. It was an old style horse-drawn cab. I'd come to town on the tram and now haggled with the cabby: how many piastres was the fare? That's the way of the world in many Eastern countries. It was all quite pleasant and friendly and soon we agreed the price. The driver in his fez and robes would make a lovely picture. As it was wartime we weren't allowed to photograph.

Inside the cab was like being in another world. Deep, dark and cushioned seating for about four. On each side of the driver were candlelit lamps. It was like being in a Victorian film. As we 'geed-up' the driver moved over and another man went up and sat beside him. This disturbed me. As we clip-clopped along the road to the docks I grew even more uneasy. When in foreign, that is non-English speaking ports, I usually tried to get a language dictionary to learn some phrases. As these two talked I gathered they were referring to me, also by their body language. Seamen were an easy target as they often had large sums of money and presents with them to take home.

The gharry turned off the main road to the docks into a shaded crescent. I asked the driver what he was doing. He said something about the lamps. One of the candles had gone out.

It wasn't too dark yet. The driver and his mate got down. I climbed out of my deep comfortable seat on to the road. The driver grabbed me by the lapels of my jacket and by then his friend had nipped round the back of the gharry. In a flash I realised he was going to strike me from behind. I ducked my head and there was a swish and a cry as he hit the driver in the face. I was released from his clutches and ran off like a bullet out of a gun.

The noise and confusion behind me gave me extra speed but no one tried to follow me. They were too busy sorting themselves out. So I escaped and along came the faithful old tram to get me safely aboard. I did not pay the cab fare but I did feel very, very angry. Here we were fighting for freedom and there were reports of Allied people being dredged out of the water daily. By the Grace of God I was not one of them. Someone, I felt, was watching over me, and someone else was out to get me. Bombs, mines, torpedoes, other nasty things and people hadn't destroyed me yet. How long could I last?

Amongst the gear I had prepared to put on for my third visit to town I had carefully prepared a small stiletto knife, sharpened and honed, to carry in a sheath attached to my right sock-suspender. Since my second escape from a mugging, or worse, I was in a state of cold rage, anger burning inside me. I felt a hatred for the 'gyppos' whom we were trying to save from the enemy. Some said they were more on the Germans' side than ours. My plan was to go to town and hire a gharry and then to get revenge on the driver and drive his horse-driven cab into the dock. Exactly how I was going to do this I didn't know. I would find a way. I usually started out with shipmates, but often came back alone. I was a survivor and, since my birth in Germany, had managed to come more or less successfully through every difficulty during my 21 years.

After going round Alexandria, the ice cream parlour, the Services Club, etc., I decided to put my plan into action. These were very violent times. It was kill or be killed. Nowhere seemed safe – even in our homes we were in danger. Life was cheap and men, women and children were daily being slaughtered. Here I was then haggling with an old man for my fare back to the ship in his gharry. I justified myself on the kill or be killed idea and that revenge was very sweet. Also he was old... We agreed the price, but it was not a very high one as he seemed to be reasonable, asking only a few piastres. As we trundled along towards the docks the driver chatted to me. His English was surprisingly good. I was completely taken off guard as he conveyed to me that he was a Christian.

This was entirely unexpected and suddenly I had flashbacks to my childhood. My German grandfather, who was a Christian, my days in Smith's Homes, Ealing, where I'd learnt Bible texts for prizes and my four years in the orphanage on Ashley Down, Bristol. I cannot remember a thing I said to him, but two things happened to me. My rage and cold planning melted. I felt a sudden surge of feeling – something like the time when I was at the bottom of the swimming pool 10 years ago at Müller's, and a warm feeling for these old, grandfather figures like the photos of my grandfather, Ernst Bremke, and George Müller came into my heart.

I was at the ship. My stiletto forgotten, I paid over the rate to the cab driver who said something encouraging to me, to which through the tempest of my feelings I could only murmur 'Thank-you and good night' as I stumbled back aboard and to my cabin. It was still about four years before I too became a Christian, but that night in Egypt began to prepare me for my personal freedom from slavery and entrance into the Kingdom of God, which was still a journey to be travelled.

Abadan to Adelaide – Phantom Torpedoes

From Alexandria we headed back through Suez, the Red Sea and the Gulf of Aden. Then we turned up into the 'Persian' Gulf, marked as the Arabian Gulf. We were making for one of the world's hot spots – Abadan. We went up the Shatt al Arab, a tributary of the Euphrates, where the Garden of Eden was sited. Our course took us through plantations of date palms and it seemed very strange to see the ships disappearing into the plantations with only their masts showing above the trees.

It was a place of truly blistering heat. All transport was free to the crews of tankers, and admission to the Club was also included. There was a swimming pool there, but immersion in the water only left us completely enervated. This was now New Year's Eve, and the Scots were preparing a big 'do' for Hogmanay. We were all invited and most of us went along.

We had a big supper in the still sweltering heat and then the usual Harry Lauder songs and entertainments. I was not given to strong drink, but preferred shandy or something very mild, as I was quite excitable enough without artificial stimulants. Just before midnight I left my large glass almost empty and went out of the room to see a fellow who was playing an accordion. Suddenly the cry went up for everyone to drink the toast to the New Year. I went back to my place and picked up my glass, which someone had re-filled in my absence. 'Bottoms up' was the cry, and many loyal toasts were called. It was evidently the custom to drain the glass at one draught. This I did, not without some difficulty, as my glass had been filled with Cognac.

That was the wildest night that I ever remember. The stuff seemed to explode in my brain like a time bomb with a very short fuse. Now I grabbed the accordion and a queue of equally inebriated servicemen formed up behind me as I led them like the Pied Piper of Hamelin. I have never played the accordion on any other occasion but this, but the effect seemed to be very good.

We trailed through the bungalows and then up onto the flat roofs, and finally down into some poor, startled fellow's bedroom, who was rudely awakened by our noisy and unannounced entry. I remember very little after that, except that I was violently sick and felt as near to dying as ever I did in my life. My face was ghastly when I peered at myself in the bathroom mirror. I was taken back to the ship by my mates, and can only remember the whole cabin rotating round my head until, on the third day, I was finally sobered, and in comparative possession of my faculties once again. We were then due to set sail, so I went back to my work more convinced than ever of the folly of strong drink.

Now we headed across the Arabian Sea to India, where we were to discharge at Bombay. It was a warm trip, relieved only by sea breezes which made it bearable.

Sea life abounded in these warm waters and we saw many large and poisonous snakes. One night we passed through a huge field of brilliantly lit phosphorescence. No one could give an explanation, but maybe it was a large school of fish that caused it to glow in that uncanny fashion.

As we neared Bombay the direction of the wind changed to an offshore breeze; the whole atmosphere underwent a transformation. The air seemed fetid and sultry. Old hands had said that you can smell Bombay a hundred miles out at sea! Now I believed them. We anchored offshore and were allowed liberty to go ashore in the afternoon. Landing at the 'Gateway of India' we were soon in the crowded streets and bazaars of that Eastern city. The place was thronged with people, cars, taxis, bicycles and cows. Two things stick out in my memory about Bombay. They are: a football match, and the kicking of a sacred cow.

The Indians on the Malabar Estate, where we discharged our cargo, challenged us to a football match one evening. They took us to the field in railway inspection cars by pushing us along the rails, running on the rails in their bare feet. The ground was hard and grassless. We played the first half with the sun at our backs and scored our first and only goal. The Indians scored a few and gave us no indication of the avalanche that was to follow once we changed ends after about half an hour. Now the sun was in our eyes and as it rapidly descended so the total of goals scored against us ascended. We lost count after the 20th, and were kindly shunted back to our ship by the jubilant locals amid many expressions of goodwill.

The kicking of the cow was not attended by such benign expressions of entente cordiale. One of the more ignorant and drunken members of our ship's crew found his path along the main road blocked by a huge and obdurate cow. As you know, the cow is a sacred animal in India, and it is a grave offence to insult it. This seaman did worse. Not content with hurling abuse at the inoffensive animal, much to the chagrin of the local bystanders, he very foolishly attacked it with the toe of his boot.

He had no difficulty in hitting such a large target at such close range, although he had been singularly unsuccessful when trying to get goals the night before! The reaction of the crowd was instant and totally expected by any but the least discerning. His senses had been impaired by the amount of local spirits he had imbibed, but now, prompted by the good advice of his companion and by the obvious intentions of the crowd, both took to their heels and made for the liberty boat. They reached the safety of the docks a fraction ahead of their pursuers and were never seen ashore again in Bombay for fear of their safety. They were in fact refused any leave and were fined for their stupid and dangerous conduct.

Our cargo was destined for Australia. We understood that there were Japanese submarines operating in the Indian Ocean, and that a number of tankers had been sunk en route to Australia.

Encouraging news for us as we headed towards
that area!. We never quite knew whether these
rumours were true, but there was a horrible possi-
bility that if not true about other ships they could
become true about us.

I had one of my biggest frights on this trip. While
sitting by myself on the 'poop', or afterdeck, one
night, I was gazing out on the bright southern sky,
admiring the Southern Cross constellation that
replaces the Great Bear polar group in the northern
hemisphere for getting one's bearings.

Suddenly my eye was diverted to a bright streak
of light which I first thought to be a comet or falling
meteorite reflected in the calm, glassy sea. As I
watched its progress I found that it was under the
water and was streaking in a straight line to about
the engine room which lay below the deck where I
was sitting. I was absolutely fixed to the spot as I
watched its swift progress straight at us. My mouth
was dry, and I remembered all sorts of things that
they said about torpedoes before they struck a ship.
It would only be a second or so before this one did
that. I stood rooted to the spot by the awful fascination of that moment. I seemed unable to move or
make a sound, but felt hypnotised as though by a
deadly snake. The phosphorescent wake showed
distinctly that it was making its way unerringly
towards us, and that nothing could now be done to
avoid it.

I felt awful that we might all be blown sky
high and here was I, seemingly helpless and use-
less. I couldn't believe that my life would end so
suddenly in the next few moments. There was so

much I had not been able to accomplish. There were so many things that needed to be put right. I would certainly cry for mercy if that blinding moment came. I would just as certainly forget all about it if it didn't! So fickle are we and so fallible in the face of crisis. Now the moment of impact was upon me.

I leant over the ship's side to watch and it seemed as though the missile suddenly took a downward turn and disappeared under the keel. I rushed to the other side of the ship and saw it surface. It was a porpoise, or some such large fish, and soon there were a number of them weaving their wisp-like trails through the luminous waters as they gambolled and played around the ship, rubbing themselves along its keel to rid themselves of the parasites that cling to them.

Later, as we neared our destination at Adelaide in South Australia, we saw a large school of whales. They were a wonderful sight to behold as they sported in the waters. They slapped their tails on the surface and made all sorts of strange noises. We felt very happy to see them and they seemed to be kindly disposed towards us.

What Happened to Pete

Pete and I shared a cabin with the second steward and as far as I remember we never fell out to any serious degree. Pete was from Shrampton (Shirehampton, near Bristol) and had lived all his life there before joining the ship at Avonmouth dock when he was 18 years old. His home had a field at the back and from there he could see the River Avon with the sights and sounds of the sea traffic moving with the tides.

He was popular and likeable; girls held a fascination for him. There were horses in the field, these attracted the girls and it was probably there that he formed an association in his mind of horses, girls and home. His mother had always looked after his clothes so he had no idea how to do washing and ironing. One day all his new clothes, except what he stood up in, got dumped in the sea.

Here's how Pete lost his clothes. He changed his clothes, always putting the soiled ones in the wardrobe. These were replaced by new ones from the suitcase. Ultimately he was faced with the fact that the suitcase was devoid of further fresh supplies. He was advised to put them in a bucket on the galley stove, and there they stayed till the cook got tired of them. After a while they grew a green culture and one of the men emptied them over the side of the ship. If you ever see any fish dressed in the latest fashion of the 1940s, be sure that they are the remnants of Pete's depleted wardrobe.

We arrived at last in Australia and visited three ports, Adelaide, Port Lincoln and Port Pirie, where our cargo of petrol was eagerly awaited. Not all the ships had got through. One ahead of us had been sunk by the Japanese in the Indian Ocean.

The country was at a standstill except for emergency services. Harvest was waiting to be gathered so most people welcomed our arrival.

We could hardly have been further from Shirehampton than in South Australia. Adelaide to be exact. But here everything seemed perfect to Pete. There was a horse on the towpath leading to the ship – hopefully soon to be homeward bound. Pete wanted to take the horse back to Avonmouth on the tanker.

While going ashore Pete expressed an interest in this rather unlikely wish. He was sober then. Our ways parted until much later in the evening.

Coming back to the ship, I noticed a field with the gate left open. I was puzzled, too, by the silhouettes in the pale sunset. The rear end of a horse and a man. Coming alongside, it was as I suspected. Pete was leading a horse along the towpath. I was certain the horse was all right, but Pete was leaning at an angle of about 45°.

'Hi Pete! Where are you going?' I said.

'To Shurrampton.'

'With the horse?'

'Yesh.'

'Why don't you ride it?'

'OK. Give ush a bunk up...'

We tried, but unfortunately neither was very experienced and only one of us was sober! Pete landed on the path at the other side of the horse. He lay perfectly still and began to breathe heavily as the evening's exertions finally took their toll. I took the halter he had so lately relinquished and led the horse back to its field, and then carried my shipmate to his bunk.

Next morning Pete was awakened with the startling news that the Skipper wanted the horse removed from 'midships as it was disturbing everyone and needed feeding and watering. The laughter that followed alerted him to the joke. We arrived back in Bristol six months later, with Pete but without the horse.

The Dream

Leaving Australia, we stocked up for our trip north to Abadan, where we loaded again and went back along the Suez route. At this time the Germans were being driven out of Southern Europe and our sailing orders came to proceed north to Italy. We passed through the Straits of Messina on our way to Naples. A wonderful view of the active volcano Stromboli gave the impression of a molten field of lava as big as a football pitch, like a beacon as we sailed by at night. Then we went past the Isle of Capri and on into the Bay of Naples. Here we saw the magnificent sight of Vesuvius, sending up puffs of smoke by day and sparks at night. No more shore leave was allowed as there was a smallpox epidemic in the city.

A storm broke over us with such ferocity that even the steel hawsers snapped and ships were in danger of being wrecked there in the harbour. The storm was soon over and by next day it seemed incredible that it had ever occurred. Due to the epidemic we were directed to unload instead at a place further along the coast. Our unloading berth was at the west end of the bay at a place mentioned in the New Testament where the apostle Paul landed on his way to Rome. It was called Puteoli in New

Testament times (now called Pozzuoli). Here we were allowed ashore.

There was certainly an air of antiquity about the place, though I wasn't so aware of it then. We went ashore and wandered into the hills and the town. There wasn't much to do so we headed back towards the ship, going down a steep hill in the brilliant light of the moon, and were able to appreciate the romantic bay dominated by the majestic silhouette of Vesuvius and the twinkling lights of the ships and the quayside below us.

A curious feature of the hill we were descending was that it had a huge hole scooped out of it as though by a giant hand. This cavernous place lay in deep shade. We were puzzled by it and stopped when we came to a gap in the hedge protecting passers-by from falling into it. The sides were stepped and I hazarded a guess that it was a disused vineyard, as there were shrubs and trees growing on the terraces.

When we reached the bottom of the hill we found a way into this rather eerie place. We found there were marble pillars, all very square and on a level with the line of the lowest terrace. In the darkness we could just make out caves also at that level and at opposite ends. I thought I could see marks of bars and scratches when we went closer to examine them.

Suddenly I saw in a blinding flash what this place was.

'It's an amphitheatre!' I yelled.

'A what?' asked my friends.

'A place where they threw the Christians to the lions,' I said.

Then I went on to tell them the other uses that the Romans made of their amphitheatres, and was surprised how much I remembered, especially about mock sea battles with real boats, all very topical to us!

Sleeping aboard the ship that night, I dreamt a terrible, yet wonderful dream.

I was on the floor of a huge arena. It was crowded with a hot, excited crowd shouting for blood. I was in the middle of the arena and around me were families of Christians – I was one of them. Lights blazed down on us so that we were not able to see clearly through the haze. Suddenly a signal was given from above, followed by a clanging open of gates. (Probably the creaking and groaning of the ship tied up!) Into the arena came wild beasts of every sort and size – lions, tigers and other carnivores that were depicted in illustrations of the early Christian martyrs. People were being torn to pieces all around me. Men, women and children.

Strange that I was not touched. Stranger still, the families dying around me seemed to be actually enjoying it. Their singing seemed to shield them like a filter. Love held them calm in the centre of all the chaos that surrounded them. Their faces were like angels. Part of their reason for rejoicing seemed to come from the crowds above them. There were voices from the terraces, calling out two words.

I would never forget those words. They were distinct and stamped on my memory. Now I woke with a start. No one shook me; it was just my time for waking.

The familiar noises of the oil tanker broke in on my consciousness as it pumped oil ashore into the storage tanks off Pozzuoli. Above us towered the hill where the amphitheatre had been scooped out – the one of my dream that we had discovered the night before. I could remember every detail of the dream – except those two words! The form of them seemed to be deep in my subconscious, and if I ever heard them again I was sure I would recognise them. Four years later I did hear them again and immediately recognised them.

I had recently become a follower of Jesus and had left the sea at the end of the war. I was in a group who were studying the Bible and Dr Willavoys read from 1 Corinthians 16 v. 22 which ends with the words *Maranatha*, which means 'The Lord comes.'

These words were shouted by other Christians at the top of the row of spectators to encourage those who were ready to die for their Lord and their faith in Him. This was hidden from me at the time of my dream, but the elements were there and it just needed the time to be fulfilled before the puzzle was revealed.

Next we did a couple of trips through Suez and back to Tarranto, in the heel of Italy, before heading across the Atlantic to New York. We berthed finally at the Naval Base in Brooklyn, a squalid district where muggings and murder were the order of things. This was my last time in New York as it turned out, and I had completed 13 return trips, making a total of 26 crossings of the Atlantic. I was now nearly 21 years of age and had a chicken in cold store to celebrate my coming of age.

Ashore Again

The day came at last for which we had worked so long. The Japanese capitulated after the dropping of the atom bombs. I was in the Suez Canal en route to Abadan.

'This is London calling. Here is the News with Alva Liddell reading it.' I stopped to listen to the crackling Tannoy system that gave a very poor reception.

'The war with Japan is over,' I thought he said, '...atom bombs were dropped on... this morning and the Japanese High Command have surrendered.' Later I learned the details. I rushed around the ship to anyone who was about and tried to tell them. No one seemed to believe me. 'Just another one gone off his head.' (Abadan was reputed to be the largest oil depot in the world and also to have the biggest mental asylum. With the heat and drink it was said that people in the oil business had 'the Abadans'. Temperatures were often over 100°F at midnight and there was a lot of cheap beer and drink at the Club.)

I soon gave up, and got on with my job. It was clear that everyone thought I was trying to 'swing the lead' and get out of my work. By midday the wireless operators got the radio tuned in to the BBC London, and my sanity was no longer questioned.

'Two atom bombs were dropped this morning, one at Nagasaki and the other at Hiroshima. The two towns were wiped out in split seconds. Thousands of Japanese killed and wounded. The Emperor and the Japanese High Command have declared a cease-fire with immediate effect, and the Allies have accepted their surrender. No more atom bombs will be dropped while the Japanese keep their word.'

However, this was not the end of my sailing days as trips continued to various ports overseas and in the UK. The final trip was round the north coast of Scotland to Aberdeen, the Granite City, and to Leith where I was paid off and had to make my own way home to Bristol.

I had given no thought to what I would do after the war. My first job was in the Beckington café in Wells, my bedroom being above Penniless Porch through which access is gained to the grounds of the Bishop's Palace and the Cathedral.

It was while working there that I heard of a vacancy in the Readers Department of the Western Daily Press. I applied and was accepted, and now at last I was to enter the Newspaper World that I had hoped to enter when only 14 years of age.

I was 25 in April 1948 and had been in the newspaper office of the Western Daily Press for nearly two years. My senior was a kind man but strict. He knew I'd been a boy in Müller's Homes and was surprised at my crudeness and unbelief. He was from a Salvation Army background and could not understand why, despite having about 10+ years in Christian Homes for children, seven in London and about four in Müller's, I was seemingly indifferent to Christianity. His cure was to lend me a copy of the autobiography of George Müller. He probably loaned it to me in an effort to improve me.

I took it home and started to read it straight away. I stayed with the first few chapters on his early life in Germany, and was surprised by the stealing, gambling, drunkenness and depravity that he indulged in, even when a theological student. I had never heard all this before. In his story he didn't elaborate on sin or give details to whet the appetite for more. How then did such a rogue get into such a position of trust and honour in a foreign land like England, and that during one of the strictest times of its history known as the Victorian era? Something must have happened to change him and it must have been very thorough and drastic.

This was a crucial part of the change about to take place in my life. I saw some parallels between his life and mine, though his search for fulfilment ended in a prayer meeting held in a butcher's shop, while I was strongly resisting any church involvement.

The war had ended and the 'lights had come on again all over the world' as the song went. I had bought a car, which I'd had to leave in a garage, as I couldn't afford to get it repaired. I had started going through various jobs as before. I was looking for promotion but prospects were not promising. I had a lovely romance with every prospect of engagement and marriage, but still I was the proverbial 'wandering star'.

The romance came about like this. I was a regular at this time at the Dance Hall called Rheads Academy and it was there that I met the most attractive girl I had seen since Mary of Philadelphia. All went remarkably smoothly at first, both with my work and with my new friendship. Phyllis was popular with everyone and friends invited us out. Even old Pop Bracey at the office said she was a stunner and I was suddenly, seemingly, a very happy man. Of course there were little frictions and disagreements, but generally we knew how to get round them.

I had kept in touch with my former schoolteacher at Müller's and had visited the old Home to show off my possessions. I was invited to this teacher's home to Sunday teas, but my arguments and opposition must have made it tough for him, his wife and three young children, to tolerate. My girlfriend was a less abrasive person and she would agree, hating any controversy, public or private. After some years of visiting Speakers' Corner in London's Hyde Park and relishing the knock-about debates, I was very irritated by her embarrassment at my taking part in public outburst or private debate. These caused the greatest strain in our relationship.

One such Sunday evening before supper and after the evening service I launched into my usual spate of arguments when Mr Andrews said, 'George, you know the truth, now let's go and have some supper.' That was it. No more argument, no getting offended or uptight, just stating what he believed to be the fact. After all, he had taught me for four years and very kindly tolerated me for about another 11 or 12 years. That short phrase 'you know the truth' rang like a bell through my head for the next two years.

I continued dancing, romancing and all the things that young couples did in the 1940s, except for sleeping together and having sex before marriage. Our romance was almost perfect. Everyone admired Phyllis and our future seemed set fair, but there was just this one fly in the ointment.

The thing that caused us to disagree violently was this matter of public debates. I had often haunted Speakers' Corner and had enjoyed all the razzmatazz of the exchanges, the wit and the repartee. The vulgarities and insults had me in stitches. Old Aunt Aggie and her Bible were gently ribbed by the students whom she solemnly warned of the consequences. Prince Monolulu was a great favourite with all the ribaldry and jokes that poured out of him. The communists were the most solemn and pompous, though secretly I was rather on their side, despite the disillusionment of earlier days. I did not fear the pickpockets when I lived in London. There was nothing in my pockets then, nor is there very often anything now.

The first time Phyllis and I went to the Bristol Speakers' Corner on the Downs I was looking forward to the knockabout of the debates as in former days. Now came the shock. I found that I was being dragged away and soon discovered that this was the surest way to a row that I could find.

I had spent the greatest part of my life in debate and discussion, but Phyllis had no such interest. At first these things were only pinpricks, but they gradually widened into the final rift that parted us, though not on the subject of politics.

We were invited to a Christmas party at Müller's Orphanage and both of us were happy to accept. I had visited the Homes a few times during the war while on leave, mainly to show them my new car and clothes. Now I discovered that these people could have great fun and I found it very much to my liking. One of the funniest parties I ever attended was the Preachers' Party. These men were not afraid to be laughed at and threw themselves into the fun and games.

I tried to explain my thoughts about God to Phyllis, but she maintained that she had never done any wrong. I might be a sinner but she was not. Talk about repentance and faith were foreign to her. She always did the best she could and she was as good as anyone else and she thought God would accept her because of this. She and her mother seemed to think that the word 'sinner' referred to a criminal. I couldn't see this at the time because I was much in the same fog myself and was trying to find my way to the light.

As I recounted these things to my girlfriend it seemed to confirm her in virtue and classify me where I belonged, among the unrighteous. I had taken the opposite line. I was a sinner – I did need, but did not yet want, to change or be changed. The battle was inside me. I was afraid and yet wanted to see the end of this struggle.

It came through another friend, Dr Willavoys, a Ph.D. in 'heavy water' – atomic energy. It was he who later unpacked the truth for me and spelt it out in direct terms, but with a lot of prayer and love. He used words like 'either you're a Christian or you're not, either you're a believer or you're not, and either you're lost or you're saved'.

Phyllis and I still continued our romance, but now with rather more intensity. Perhaps we sensed it was doomed to failure and we were trying to preserve the cherished dream. I was by nature an enquiring, argumentative character and I found her dislike of debate and discussion was becoming a barrier to our reaching any understanding. Hostile silence and active disapproval are not conducive to finding a solution to one's problems. My friend, Dr Willavoys, invited us to a meal and although we had both accepted, Phyllis refused to go at the last minute.

Walking towards The Centre, Bristol, soon after, I spotted the Doctor coming towards me, and darted quickly down a back street. What a strange state my mind was in. What was happening to me? I decided to write and apologise for not turning up at the meal, and then, as I had no arguments of my own left, went on to put Phyllis's point of view as though it were mine. I felt that this letter was my swan song and that I would then bow myself out, or...? Once posted, the letter assumed great importance. The expected reply did not come. I waited a week. Still silence. Two weeks went by without a word.

Saved – the Prodigal Returns

In my spare time I worked on my car and a motor bike that I had bought. A friend from the newspaper office had promised to help me get the bike in good working order as it had lain idle for some time. I had rented an old shed for garaging both vehicles and the shed owner was painting my car.

It was a beautiful June morning. Just two years after the Second World War. My friend from the Western Daily Press was coming at 9.00 a.m. to sort out my motorbike – a 250 cc Sunbeam. I picked up the letter on the mat as I went out to the garage across the road in Clifton.

Sam was prompt, turning up at exactly 9.00 a.m., and he said, 'I've got to leave early, about a quarter to 12.'

'That's fine Sam,' I said. Actually I wished he would go earlier as the letter I'd been waiting for was 'burning a hole in my pocket'. It had been over two weeks in coming. We worked away on the engine of the bike, chatting about motorbikes with the occasional 'swear word'. I didn't want to use one – rather unusual for me as I boasted I could swear for two minutes without repeating myself. I was now 25 and the Merchant Navy service of over five years had left its mark on me.

At 11.45 we packed up. Sam got on his bicycle and rode off home. I sat on the running board of the Hillman Saloon and carefully opened my letter. Although it was a warm June day – the 6th to be precise – I found I was shivering! Was it fear, anticipation, or what? The writer was a very kind and gentle man called Dr Henry Willavoys who was Vice Principal of the Technical College (now called City of Bristol College). He wrote about being 'lost' or 'saved'. Those two words meant something to me. Years at sea had taught me what the word 'lost' meant. Suddenly I felt as though I was back at sea.

A tanker on fire on a dark night in the North Atlantic is a fearful sight – especially as I was on an oil tanker with 4 million or so gallons of petrol and oil aboard. The dark outline of the burning ship in a sea of fire made me feel sick. The explosions and shooting flames lighting up the whole convoy of 30–40 merchant ships plus four or five escort destroyers were sitting ducks for the U-boats – submarines prowling around and sometimes surfacing in the middle of the convoy.

All this and more flashed before me as I read the words 'lost' or 'saved' and I knew I was lost. It was as though time stood still. All my present hopes and fears, my ambitions and desires were completely suspended. Now the word of God came clearly to me. Christ came to save. I needed to be saved from myself, my sins and from the just punishment of them – only One could save me. His name meant Saviour.

Here was I in a tumbledown garage, sitting on a decrepit car, reading Eternal Truths. I could do nothing to help myself. What a joyous letter of love it was. Jesus loved ME; did I love HIM? You either accept and receive Him, or you reject Him.

When I started reading I was trembling. I felt I was on the edge of a great event. Sitting there on the running board of my car, I knew, in a blinding flash, that I was SAVED.

Then it seemed as though a great and mighty hand scooped me up clear of all my fears and doubts and filled me with a happiness and contentment I had never known. Like a brilliant flash in that dark place, there came the Truth I'd sought so long. It was the Lord. Not an abstract teaching but God himself in the person of his Son. I was enraptured. Nothing else counted as my soul fused into His presence. I was sealed to Him by the divine seal of his Holy Spirit. I'd done nothing to deserve this marvellous love. It was all pure Grace. It flowed into me as though a liquid balm were poured into my troubled and wounded soul. In a moment I was healed, restored, forgiven and bursting to sing His praises.

As I continued sitting in that gloomy place my whole being was aglow. All my doubts and fears were gone. The searching, the questioning, were at an end.

Just then I was brought back to earth by the chimes of Great George striking twelve in the tower of Bristol University. I rose, putting the letter in my pocket, and crossed the road back to my lodgings. I ran upstairs and burst into the kitchen where Mrs Dillon was preparing dinner.

'Mrs D,' I said, 'I've been converted. I've become a Christian.'

'Give it three months,' said the wise Mrs Dillon. 'You've been about everything else I can think of since I've known you, C of E, Catholic, Communist!'

Thirty years later, when she was 90, she said, 'You got the real thing that time, George.' She too had become a Christian, rather to the puzzlement of some of her family.

I began to realise I would have to live out my conversion here on earth among the very people whom I had counted as my friends and who might now regard me as 'strange'. They would test my confession and they would judge for themselves as to its reality. But now it was time for dinner, and later I had a date to keep with Phyllis. I didn't know how she would take this news, but it didn't worry me. I was prepared for whatever would be the outcome.

I was not insensitive. I loved her and wanted to marry her, but nothing would shake me from this thing that had happened to me. At that moment I would gladly have gone, like the martyrs of old, to die rather than give up my faith, or to deny my Lord. Nothing could entirely separate me from God's love. The love I had could grow dim and clouds would come and go, but the fact was established for ever.

I read the letter through again. I knew what had happened. I was changed. It was as Jesus explained to Nicodemus, that unless you are born again and become as a little child you cannot enter the Kingdom of God. I was born again – a child of God.

My mind seemed to be so clear and I was uplifted in spirit, soul and body. I had tasted the Elixir of Life. There was no hangover to follow. A mellowing, yes; also a deepening as experience followed upon the thrill that had captured my soul. The sin-barrier that had circumscribed me had been broken by a mightier hand than mine. It was a nail-pierced hand and I was conscious that those were the wounds of Divine Love. Greater than any love I had ever felt for another human being. Greater love than I had ever imagined could exist. I had faintly glimpsed this love over the 25 years of my life so far. It was brightest and very near to me the day I was on the bottom of the swimming pool as a boy. I detected its nearness at other times of crisis when the fear of death was upon me. I knew that I had but to call out or stretch out my hand and it would be mine. Yet I had neglected and refused that Love for so long. Such is the patience of the Lord Jesus.

George aged 25

Dancing

'Let's go to Rhead's on Saturday evening.' The young people who went ballroom dancing were very friendly. Nothing formal, only the girls and a few older fellows wore special clothes. At first Phyllis was reluctant to go. She was the youngest of three sisters, working at home, and with a few local jobs helping elderly or disabled neighbours. One of her older sisters came along with us and she brought her boyfriend, who felt a little out of place as he was a mechanic, not an office-type like most of the others.

'The boys and girls are very nice,' they assured their parents. I worked in a newspaper office in Bristol, had a car and was living in a flat in Clifton with a family who had given me board and lodging. I left the sea at the end of the war, and was a regular at the dance hall. I had no girlfriend there until I met Phyllis. Then we went as a foursome, when Stan could be persuaded. 'It's all right, they're not snobs, just young people like ourselves,' we told him.

There was a small 'live' band on stage. I soon got friendly with them. Mr Rhead the owner never seemed to have any special friends, he was always there as MC. When he was busy the bandleader took over. This was the age of ballroom dancing in the 1940s. Foxtrots, Waltzes and Tangos were the 'in thing', although the Americans had introduced jitterbugging and other less graceful forms of dancing before they went back to the U.S.A. after the armistice in 1946. The girls generally were keen on the American ways.

Two dances were very popular during the evening's programme. They were the 'excuse me' dance and the 'ladies' invitation'. These happened at least once during an evening and were especially popular after the 'interval' of half-an-hour. Most went out for a drink in one of the local pubs. It was reckoned by some that the dancing never really got going until after the interval.

The dance floor had small tables and chairs on three sides. Soft drinks, etc., could be bought, but there was no licence for selling alcohol.

'If you want dancing lessons, Mr Rhead or Mr Shaw can give them on Wednesdays or by arrangement.' I seem to remember picking mine up from the girls at the dance, and from my landlady's daughter.

She was older than I was, but there was no love lost between us. She soon made it very obvious that I was not welcome and things came to a head one day between her and the family when Bobby, the youngest son, found me packing my bags to leave. I shared a room with Bill and Bobby in the rather large basement flat in Victoria Square, Clifton.

'If George is going,' he said angrily, 'then I'm going too.' That settled the matter, much to Mrs Dillon's relief. She didn't want me to go, neither did

Bill, the older son. So an uneasy truce was reached. I was never quite accepted by Eileen, although I kept in touch with the family until Mrs Dillon's death some 30 years later. I still see Bill occasionally – when passing his house I sometimes drop in for a cup of tea and a chat – especially about cricket.

And so it was that on the first Saturday of June 1948 I experienced the most complete change in my life. From 12 noon on that lovely sunny day I became a Christian. I had an irresistible compulsion to tell everyone I met that I had changed. It could not have felt better if I'd won the biggest lottery in the world. I've never lost that compulsion but have tempered it with prayerful discretion. Mrs Dillon was the first to know, and then I went to meet Phyllis as we arranged for that evening. I told all her family, who were rather overwhelmed. The reaction was 'Poor Phyllis, her boyfriend has got "religious mania".' But years later I believe that some of them also accepted Christ.

You may be able to guess what happened. I told everyone I met, from Mr Rhead on the door, to the band players, and to the other dancers, at some time or other, sooner or later: 'Did I tell you I became a Christian on 6th June at midday?' I would say.

Phyllis did not like what was happening, nor did my friends in the dance hall on the first occasion since my conversion. So when we came back after the interval from the local pub, where I'd had a wonderful chance to share my 'secret' in the bar amidst all the smoke and noise, Mr Rhead called me aside. 'George,' he said, 'everyone is complaining about you preaching at them. Either you stop or you'll have to leave until you can stop upsetting and spoiling the dancers' evening.'

'Well Mr Rhead, I'm sorry they've taken it like that. After all, I was only telling them what has happened to me, and I wanted them, and of course you, to also enjoy being "converted". You see it was like this...' At that point Mr Rhead stopped me.

'There you are, you're starting to preach to me. I'm sorry but you'll have to go, and don't come back again unless you can change your ways.' I never did go back, but I have been trying to learn some 'sanctified common-sense'.

Phyllis had already left the Academy and was waiting to go home by my car. It was a tense journey across the City and not a very happy early return home. She disappeared into the kitchen and cried in her mother's arms. I felt so miserable. I readily agreed when her mother wisely advised, 'It is best if you leave her alone, until you sort yourselves out.' This was one of the four times we parted, until her mother finally said to her, 'You might as well stop seeing each other, if he goes to work in a children's home and wants to go to foreign lands to work.' Her final letter said 'either you go halfway with me or...' I answered her letter while she was staying in Falmouth for a month with some of their church-going friends. My reply was 'Jesus went all the way to Calvary for me (and died to set me free) and I want to go all the way with him. There is no "halfway house". If you are willing to go all the way then we can go together. If not then I have no other choice. I'm sorry but that's exactly how it is.' Even today I feel the sadness for her, myself, and her family, but also the gladness that I was given the strength and by the love of God have continued to rely on His faithfulness. (I only ever saw her once again a few years later when we had both married and had our own families.)

Some years later one of Phyllis's family wrote and told me that my conversion had deeply affected them, and they had admired my sincerity, she added that God had been good to her over the years. Jesus did not promise us an easy life if we followed Him. Even his own mother, brothers and sisters thought him mad. On one occasion they wanted to take him forcibly – presumably for his own good! Jesus said, 'Whoever prefers [or chooses] others before me is not worthy of me'(NIV).

I continued to feel sad about parting with Phyllis and her family, but now felt I must put Jesus first as my Saviour and Lord. Actually, Mr Andrews did pray with us after one Sunday evening service, but from that time on there seemed to come a parting of our ways. There was no turning back. I had decided to follow Jesus.

Is It Real?

With my new lifestyle there were many things to learn.

There was one test that I was sure would confirm that my new faith was real. I felt that if the Communion service at Bethesda Church, which I had attended as a boy, meant something to me now, I would know that it was real. So many of my friends suggested that either it was not, or that I was suffering some kind of hallucination, that I needed some point of reference, and this was it.

When I went to Great George Street, off Park Street, I discovered that the old Bethesda had been burnt down in the blitz. Fortunately I found out before Sunday, so was able to phone a friend who told me that there was a similar chapel called Bethesda in Alma Road. On Sunday morning I got up early and cycled there for about 9.00 a.m. only to learn that the Communion service would start at 11 o'clock, so back I went to my lodgings and read a Bible that I'd unearthed from somewhere. As I was meditating on it I fell asleep, then woke with a start to find that it was already 11.00 a.m. I hastily brushed myself down and got on my bike again and found the service well underway when I arrived.

Late and a little dishevelled, I sat down in the back row and was soon lost in the service. I followed it with rapt attention, and I understood what had always been shrouded in mystery for me as a boy. The service moved simply and majestically to the consummation when one of the worshippers went to the table and gave thanks for the loaf of bread, representing the body of Christ, which was broken for us.

As he did this I knew that it was absolutely true for me. He died for me. His body was given for me. The plate was passed round, but I did not take the bread. It was, in a sense, not essential for me at that moment. A prayer of thanksgiving was offered and the wine was poured into the cup and passed from hand to hand. It was all so familiar, yet it was all so wonderfully new as for the first time my soul was thrilled with the new significance of this moving feast of love.

Mr Melville Capper, the surgeon, then read about attempting to remove the speck from your brother's eye, while ignoring the plank in your own eye, then spoke gently about not criticising others.

He was a big, rugged man and his fingers looked so capable as he spoke of the delicate operation of removing a speck from an eye, and how foolish to attempt it with a plank in your own. I waited till the collection plate had been passed and then slipped out. I was doubly sure. I had never doubted that I was truly born again, but here was the confirmation that came from the Lord's request to his followers that they remember his death and coming to life again, until he returns for us.

It was sometime later that I first took the bread and wine. I was happy to wait until I was baptised so that I had opportunity to learn more of the significance of what I was doing. The New Testament instructs us to examine ourselves before we take Communion. I did that and still do, whenever I go to remember the Lord. It is a solemn exercise and yet, when done sincerely, one that brings great joy and blessing.

Another thing I needed to learn was what really constituted faith. I had been rather generous one day and found myself late for an appointment and without money. I hailed a taxi and asked to be taken to my lodgings. I fully believed that I would somehow receive the money for the fare as George Müller did when he needed money. As the taxi sped across the city, an awful feeling of doubt came over me. Was I right to expect to receive money for this taxi when I was strong and healthy and the lateness was due to my own bad timing? The taxi stopped outside my destination. I fumbled in my pockets and found what I knew I would. Nothing. Not one penny. I would have to go and borrow from the poor widow who was my landlady.

This was a lesson on presumption and it was dramatically impressed on me. Another day I left my bicycle outside a swimming bath, trusting the Lord to look after it for me, despite the notices about locking it up. It was stolen, of course. The police later found it and also the culprit, and the sergeant pointed out to me that I was guilty of putting temptation in the way of someone.

A service for believer's baptism was arranged and I was very keen to be baptised. It was a warm evening, so I anticipated the cool, clear water with some relish, and after the 10 girls were baptised I was the first of three men to go into the water. Did I believe? I believed with all my heart, soul and body.

Then, as I came up out of the water, the singing broke over me like an angel choir. 'Buried with Christ and raised with him too, what is there left for me to do? Simply to cease from struggling and strife, simply to walk in newness of life.' Following my baptism I was received as a member of my local church, and began to use the gifts the Holy Spirit had given me, and also to receive from others as they used their gifts to miniser to me.

Special Delivery

'Do you mind if I call you by your first name, Mr Collett?'

'No Sir, I don't mind. As you know, it's George.'

'I need someone to help me to deliver the First Editions to Gloucester after the paper comes off the press, George. What time do you finish in the Proof Reading Department?'

'At about 2.30 to 3.00 a.m. tonight, or rather tomorrow...' I replied. I was unsure whether I should call him Sir, Mr Shapcott or Sam!' So I left a space.

I was hoping he wanted me to take his car, a lovely open tourer, up the A38, but no, as his next remark showed.

'I'm taking them up in my car and I need someone to help me load and unload. What time do your people expect you back home?'

'I have a key, and my landlady never questions about what time I get in. I've been lodging with her family for nearly two years now.'

'Mrs D' (for Dillon) was a widow. Her husband left her with four young children many years ago. She had three sons and a daughter and I was part of the family now. So about 3.00 a.m. on a warm summer's morning in 1950 the Editor and I set off north to Gloucester to deliver the First Edition. Why it had missed the usual delivery from Temple Meads I never thought to enquire. Our return journey took about two hours with a break for coffee in Gloucester City.

It was a couple of months since my life had changed so dramatically and I found night work had become a problem. Having to go into work in a newspaper office early in the evening was bad enough when I wasn't a churchgoer, but when I had only one out of four Sundays off, to go into the office made it worse. Phyllis and I had coped with this for 1½ years because we could spend the afternoon and early evening together before I hopped on my bike or in the car to go into town.

Since my life had changed I now wanted to attend church and especially the after-church young people's 'squashes', with or without Phyllis, but I could only do that on my once-a-month Sunday off.

The Editor had suggested that one of the others in the 'Readers Room' could change shifts with me. There were only four of us with a substitute for absences. I thought about this and prayed about it, as my former Master/Teacher at Müller's Homes advised me. He, Mr Andrews, and Dr Henry Willavoys were Elders in the Church of Ebenezer, Filton Avenue, where I had just been baptised by immersion as a Believer. Now I felt it was unfair to expect someone to work an extra night, as that would prevent them attending church if they wanted to.

Mr Shapcott knew all this because I took up the corrected proof for his daily 'Leader' article around midnight each evening. I usually sat and waited at his desk, while he checked it through and asked any questions. He often chatted with me and knew that I had been in the Merchant Navy for 5½ years. Also he was quite interested in the fact that I was a former Müller's Boy, but up to that time – early summer 1948 – I was not a regular church attender. Then came this extraordinary request to become free to go to church. He listened to a short account of how I had changed, but we always broke off at the most interesting point of his questioning as the article had 'to go to bed', or the paper would be late for the London and country editions. This was our deadline.

This two-hour return journey to Gloucester was evidently a ruse of Mr Shapcott's to give me an extended interview. For me it was a golden opportunity to tell him how this 'conversion' came about.

'Have you got another job yet, George?' the Editor asked me as we drove along.

'Not yet, but I'm sure the Lord has something for me if he's saved me, Sir.' I was 25 and he was about 10 years older. I knew very little about him. He knew a lot about me – he had engaged me in the first place on the recommendation of my senior, 'Pop' Bracey. I had been given a brief interview by S. Shapcott and a Mr Passmore and got the job starting that weekend as a copyholder at £2.50 a week. My lodgings cost me about half of that.

He already knew that I had an ambition to work in journalism, even as a boy in Müller's Homes. He had also read my letter to the Director of the Homes, which was published that year in their

Annual Report. But now I had given two weeks notice to leave the W.D. Press.

'Have you got a job?' was his repeated question. I think he suspected I might be going over to the Evening World or the Evening Post. Some had done that recently.

'No, I haven't, but I'm not worried.'

'Well then, what will you do if you don't get one by Friday?' That was when my notice ran out – just a couple of days away. Everyone seemed worried about it – except me, ever the optimist.

'I don't know yet. I am praying about it. I did read that "The Lord would provide", and I am waiting and expecting him to answer my prayers.'

'What do you expect, and what do you want to do then George?'

'Well, anything that he shows me he wants me to do.'

As we neared Bristol he said, 'I'll be very interested to see what happens.'

'Thank you,' I said, 'You can drop me off anywhere convenient.'

'Oh that's all right, I'm passing through Clifton, so I'll leave you near the Vic Rooms.'

'Thanks very much, I live in Frederick Place, nearby.'

Friday night was a strange experience. Everyone wanted to know what I was going to do. My girlfriend, friends, landlady and family and of course people at the 'Press'. Even my church friends were concerned. Was I being 'sensible'?

'You know God does expect us to do something as well as to blindly trust him', some suggested.

'God may feed the birds,' as Jesus said, 'but he doesn't line them all up and drop it into their open beaks!' I had no answers, even at midnight when the Editor had scanned through this final article. He tipped his chair back before handing me the paper. 'So you've got your final pay-packet, George.'

'Yes I have, thank you Sir.'

'And still you have nowhere to go next week?'

'That's right!' I was not downcast or discouraged. In fact I was elated, lifted up as though I was expecting to discover something wonderful. It was just before midnight and I hadn't the slightest idea what God would do.

Leaning across the table, Mr Shapcott with his freckled face and auburn hair asked me, 'What would you say if we offered you a daytime job working under me, organising all our books, papers, etc., and producing a catalogue and cross-reference?'

I replied, 'I've never done that work before, but if I can go to the Central Library and study their system, and all else being equal, I would be willing, Sir.'

'Thank you George. You can start on Monday at 9.00 a.m. and your salary will be £3.00 per week. You will be responsible to me alone and you will have the present Library, which is a shambles, and when that is catalogued and completed, we can discuss where to go from there. Your holidays and all staff privileges are the same. Come and go as you please.'

In a flash I saw this was the Lord's answer to my prayers. I had already done some sorting and cataloguing in the Editor's Office, especially of the photos, etc., from the concentration camps at Auchswitz and Buchenwald, and elsewhere.

'Thank you sir. Do you want me to answer now?'

'No, you can go away and think about it, discuss it with your friends and then I'll see you on Monday about 10.00 a.m. to hear your final decision.'

'I'm pretty sure it will be "yes", but I'll take your advice, Sir!'

'Good. I'll see you then.' He shook hands with me and as I left the room he made one parting remark, 'I'm not altogether clear about this "conversion" business, but I wish a few more round here would get it!'

The Prodigal Goes Home

Looking back, my life had dramatically changed. From being an unbelieving critic to becoming a true Christian took about 12 years. During that time I had lived through stormy times. A number of people had wanted to adopt me from the ages of 14 to 18. I had refused up to five different people, and had survived bombings in London and Bristol, and then over five years at sea in the Merchant Navy.

Now the whole of my life was turned around. All my old arguments had gone. All my life was changed. I had become a child of God. From that moment on I started a new life. That wasn't the end, but only the beginning. What was I going to do about all the things in my life of 25 years? What about my job? I wanted to be in journalism. That was my ambition – or a teacher? And there were others. Would I split up with my girlfriend and would I go back into Müller's Homes as a teacher? Both in fact happened.

My teacher friend asked me if I would consider helping for two weeks at a holiday home owned by Müller's at Minehead, where he was taking 30 boys with his family. Yes, I felt this was good. There were so many changes taking place in my life, and this proved to be a stabilising factor. I knew Müller's; they knew me.

On a walk along the beach one fine September afternoon I was surprised that one of the Directors, Mr McCready, a very kind soft-spoken Scotsman, wanted to talk with me. As we talked Mr McCready dropped a bombshell. Would I prayerfully consider coming back to Müller's to help as an Assistant House and Sports Master? He suggested I give it time and let him know by a certain date. How could I know?

I discussed it with Mr Andrews and he suggested that I should read the Bible – especially the New Testament stories about how Jesus called his disciples to follow and work with him. He thought I would be very suitable and would pray for me. I was perhaps a little afraid of the thought, but went ahead anyhow. Finally I was told that the Directors would like to hear from me soon and could I give them an answer?

I was reading at that precise time how Jesus cast out the demons possessing the man called Legion. That was wonderful, but the sting was in the tail – when he asked Jesus if he could follow him as he travelled. Jesus said, 'Go home and show them what great things the Lord has done for you.' Home for me was Müller's. Could I face it, could I survive and still be the person I felt I should be? I preferred to go anywhere else.

Then came the message, 'The Directors would like a reply by the weekend.'

Kneeling at the washbasin in my lodgings, I groaned before God. As I kneeled there, passing through chaotic feelings of joy, fear, and all between, I suddenly saw an opening in front of me. Like the door when I was drowning – but different. The place beyond was filled with a glowing robe. Round the edges were bells and pomegranates. I recognised that this was the garment of the great High Priest of the Old Testament. The whole space was filled and I looked up to see who was in it. There was no end to the height or depth. It covered Heaven and earth.

I bowed down in fear and joy – reverence you might say, and then I felt as though a very gentle, loving hand was placed on my head. No word was spoken, no sound heard. But I knew that the thing I had feared most was exactly what I was to do. The message seemed to be: 'Go, and I am with you.' I went and when I have continued to obey, there has not been the slightest fear or doubt in my mind all these years.

I had now to leave my job and my lodgings and go to live at the Orphan Homes. The process of the preceding years was reversed. I had left as an uncertain boy, but full of good intentions, now I returned as a man and a committed Christian, again full of good intentions. I was well known in the orphanage. My name was in the punishment book for various offences! I was no nine-day wonder to them, but the way my life had changed was a cause for rejoicing and praise to God.

The boys, however, would regard me as their natural enemy and they were about 100 to one. I had met some of them at Müller's Holiday Home in Minehead and they understood that I was an old boy from No. 4 house and that I knew their language and their ways from experience.

About the first thing I did at Minehead with Mr Andrews and the 30 lads in his party, was to catch a boy disappearing out of a window. I leaned over and placed a well-aimed smack dead centre of the patch in the seat of his trousers. He leaped round and shouted out, 'Look out freshie!' to which I replied without thought, 'I'll give you a thick ear if you call me a freshie, you dinkie.' A howl of laughter went up from the boys beside me, and the lad outside (called Beale – or was it Trengrove – both were very cheeky boys just as I had been) said, 'Hey! He knows our lingo,' and that was my first test passed.

But then I had to live with them all for six more years! My special responsibility was to be games and sports as well as the other normal duties that everyone had to do.

About Girls and Marriage

The majority of boys and girls who lived on Ashley Down and who return to the Annual Reunions have had stable, long-term marriages. Despite the general lack of knowledge of the pattern of today's 'relationships', marriage for them has meant 'for life'. There are always the exceptions, as in every group. The Müller family, one of the largest ever to have been brought up in Bristol, now numbers many hundreds of thousands. George and Mary Müller had no grandchildren, but have an abundance of spiritual descendants. Among over 18,500 during the history of the Müller's Homes, the majority married, and their children are part of that same Müller family.

'How can I be sure that I can find the right partner for me, for the rest of my life?' This was the question I asked my colleague and my former teacher, Mr W.H. Andrews, 'Bert' to his contemporaries – after I had gone back to work as a House Master at 25 years of age.

I had met girls in seaports from the USA to Australia, in South America, Africa and wherever we docked, generally through Services Clubs and Seamen's Mission Socials. While in New York I became friendly with an English family. I had met the daughter at the Services Club in Manhattan and I went to dine with them in their luxury apartment. They had a West Indian cook who was an excellent chaperone. Her English roast beef was the rarest and bloodiest offering I had ever been introduced to. I felt I needed the highball before dinner to give me courage to face the surgical operation before me on the plate. I rather disappointed the cook and the girl was one of the most colourless I had ever met!

Another girl invited me to meet her family; she was the daughter of a surgeon. I arrived at the appointed time and was again admitted by a West Indian cook. There were two girls in this family and the one I had dated was not a patch on her vivacious sister, who shouted her greetings from the shower while I was being regaled with Coke and cookies in the lounge.

'Don't go away,' she pleaded, 'I want to meet your English boy.' We got on rather wonderfully once she was presentable, but of course I couldn't capitalise on it as I was already dating her sister. Like ships passing in the night, we never met again. But now at 25 I was still single.

Until I was 18 I was almost totally ignorant of anything to do with sex, not knowing anything more than even the most obvious physical differences between male and female. Then I was introduced to Dr Marie Stopes' book, *Love, Sex and Marriage*, I think it was called. Some years later I read Mr Melville Capper's book *Heirs Together* which at least gave drawings (not that I could understand them all), but it also gave a biblical Christian viewpoint which was very much in line with what I wanted, more than just the physical or romantic emphasis of secular books. Not that these were omitted, in fact their importance was fully explained, but they weren't the main thrust – not the whole story.

I believe we are made in God's image, in three parts – body, soul and spirit. Our spirit is of equal importance with our soul and body, and needs to be alive, if we are to be balanced, whole people.

I began to realise that sex is God's idea. He planned for our enjoyment so that we should have the desire to reproduce, but it needs to be entered into according to His (the Maker's) instructions, if we are to get the greatest enjoyment and benefit together. God's ideal of marriage, between one man and one woman for life is for our well being and protection, and also for that of our children.

We do not live in an ideal world (Jesus refers to this in Matthew 3:3–9) but as far as at all possible it is good to preserve marriage and family life as the best way of nurturing each generation. The legal aspect of it is not 'just a piece of paper' but a valid way of announcing to the community in which we live that this woman and this man belong to each other and are not available to anyone else. Adultery is stealing. We are quick to protect our homes and our cars from theft, so why not each other? To ignore boundaries and guidelines is to court disaster.

I was inquisitive about this whole subject, and going to sea did not at first help or teach me. Much of the conversation was about girls and the language was crude. I learnt to swear, and also a lot of jokes, but until about a year and a half after I joined the Merchant Navy, I was no wiser than before. I did learn pretty quickly that the jokes and words were not acceptable in polite company.

On a very long trip of about a year I got friendly with a steward on the ship who was also a medical orderly. He was incidentally a practising Christian and for that reason alone I avoided him socially. There's not a lot of choice for making friends among your shipmates when there are only 40 to 50 crew. The number was greatly reduced because of the different departments: officers, engineers, deck, catering and wireless. We were both in catering.

Gradually we got to know each other and he learnt about my upbringing. He was an intelligent, laid-back kind of person, not much older than I was but a lot more knowledgeable about the world's ways, medical matters and sex.

'But Dave,' I said one day, 'What's wrong with going with these girls that came to us in the café today? As long as they don't have a baby, surely that's not wrong?' I added.

'Well, I disagree, but I won't go into that now because I know you don't believe that last statement. Your upbringing in Germany and in the Children's Homes in the United Kingdom taught you that, as well as the churches and church school.' He wasn't against sex, but – and here was the crunch – 'There are hidden dangers which you have not realised, George.'

He mentioned a father and son who had gone to a brothel in Buenos Aires and had been put ashore in New York as they both had the same disease –

'VD, that is the hidden danger,' he said. The father and son did not reach home in the United Kingdom until a month later than their shipmates. They had spent a month on Ellis Island off New York and had to pay for a month's expensive and painful cure. Their wives and families were told they had caught a tropical disease.

I had never heard about this before in detail. I'd heard the term, but did not understand exactly what it meant. Dave explained it to me. Further he explained how one could prevent catching it.

'The obvious thing is don't go with a prostitute.' I didn't ask him if he had. He knew that I hadn't.

'But if you can't keep away, I'll give you something to guard against making a girl pregnant or getting VD' (now called sexually transmitted diseases including Aids). I was a very interested pupil and I have thanked God for Dave's advice to me.

So how did God answer my prayer about who to marry? I made the usual mistakes, always believing that if I were wrong God would somehow bail me out. In various ways he did. After leaving the Merchant Navy I joined a growing, lively church where there were lots of young men and girls. It wasn't long before I got friendly with one of the girls. She asked me: 'Would you like to come to tea?'

Very soon I found that I was really back to my old ways of flirting. 'Mr Andrews, do you think I should stay single in case I wanted, or was called, to become a missionary?' A popular misconception – especially as nearly every male missionary was married and some with quite large families!

'Well, no George, I don't think you're cut out for a monk's life. You do need to pray that you will know God's will both for the one you choose to marry and for yourself.'

'Well, what about the girl from our church that I'm friendly with now?'

'She's a very good person, but you have to know more about each other and find out if you are ready to commit yourselves to each other and to God.'

'I don't feel that about her, but I think she does about me. What would you advise?' This was our conversation in the Master's sitting room while on duty with my colleague, and former schoolteacher, following similar discussions at his home when out to a meal.

'If you feel that strongly, then you might consider not going any further, and you could gently discuss that with her.' That is what happened.

She seemed prepared to give up our friendship right away – and then shortly afterwards became friendly and married one of my best friends who had been too shy to approach her! He was also a former Müller's boy and they have a lovely family and are still together as far as I know.

Where does that leave me? Mr and Mrs Andrews had often invited me to Müller's Christmas parties when I was on leave from the Merchant Navy. I loved to go so that I could show off my car, motorbike or anything else. At these huge affairs I had noticed some very attractive guests – 'outsiders' connected with the Homes – two teenage girls in particular noticeable by their plaits. Not being a Christian at that time, I instinctively knew that I

would not ask for a date. But still, they were very
attractive.

In Search of a Partner

After dating several girls rather aimlessly, my senior colleague and friend, Mr Andrews, gave me some very wise advice.

'Before you ask any of the young women on the staff, George, you would do well to pray about your choice.'

'But how will I know the answer?' I asked. 'Can I look for a sign?'

'Yes, certainly – from the girl, and if necessary from the Lord,' he said with a twinkle in his eye that I had known as a boy in his class some 12 years before.

I knew that if I asked any of the girls on the staff to be my guest at our Christmas party, everyone would soon know about it. I'd already made that mistake at least once, before returning to work at Müller's a year ago. There was one girl that I vaguely thought I might like to ask, but there was nothing very strong about our acquaintance. She was an 'outsider' coming from a distance to work among the children, but trained, unlike me, who had no qualifications except that of being an 'old boy'. I was poacher turned gamekeeper.

Invitations were sent through the internal mail and everyone understood the meaning. The day to send the invite had come. So with all this on my mind, I did what my senior colleague suggested and took my Bible as I knelt down at 5.30 a.m. before going on duty to waken the boys in the dormitories.

My reading was not in a promising place. The book of Jeremiah. Still this was the chapter for the day. It was amazing.

Verse one reads 'The word of the Lord came to me.'

Verse two, 'You must not marry and have sons or daughters in this place.' Jeremiah is blamed sometimes for what he heard and wrote, but the 'Notes' pointed out that that was what the Lord God said and, like me, Jeremiah either had to listen and obey or do his own thing. So that was it. I got up from my knees and went out to get the boys out of bed. 100 boys between the ages of 11 and 17 do not leave you much time or energy to argue with the Lord.

Later, when Mr Andrews came in to teach in the school, I told him and he nodded wisely and said, 'I'm not surprised. God has his own way of answering our prayers – and his own time.'

I was invited to other parties, mainly of young church-going people and it was at one of these that I met Ruth and Jean, two sisters, and very much like the two girls with plaits I had seen at a Müller's Party.

This time I knew in my heart that Ruth, the younger one, was the one that I loved, and also that she was free – but she was training at the London Foot Hospital. Jean was friendly with Gerald, a medical student from Newport in Wales.

Ruth was of Irish parentage, her father being from Ulster and her mother from Eire. They were part of the Protestant minority group in Eire and worshipped in a similar fashion to that practised by George Müller and others in Bristol. The family had had to come to England because of the persecution there and especially to Bristol because of their interest in the work of George Müller. So here we were, both refugees from the oppressors, religious and political. When we first met I was assistant to the master who was MC for the evening. I was very much attracted to Ruth and found that she was also the cousin of one of the Sunday School teachers, so I asked her cousin to keep me a place next to them, as I had to see the boys to bed before I could join them.

When I entered the dining room later I was delighted to find that a place had been reserved for me, and soon I was enjoying hot sausage rolls and other party fare. While sitting together, Ruth asked me what the piece of Chinese writing on the wall meant, and I was able to answer, 'Ask, then certainly obtain.' It was a translation from the Bible, which says 'Ask, and it will be given to you.' I felt sure that this advice was being given to me too, and certainly took it as such. (Incidentally, the dining room had once been Mr Müller's Prayer Room.)

We met again at another party. I was rather late going and had almost decided I was too tired. I found there was no one there of special interest and I was wondering how soon I could decently leave, when the door opened and the two sisters came in. Thoughts of leaving the party now vanished from my mind. Looking into the face of the younger of the two girls my heart skipped a beat. It was Ruth, tall and slim and with an air of calmness and assurance about her. The sisters had been elsewhere that evening and this was their second port of call. They were not able to stay late as their father was ill, neither could I stay as I had to relieve the master on duty. However, I wrote to her and we met whenever she was home from her studies in London.

Ruth and I had an on-off relationship at first. Her life was governed by studying in London and helping to look after her elderly father when home in Bristol, and mine by my duties at the orphanage. I had so much to learn as a Sports Master, but I really did enjoy it. I was given a free hand to buy equipment and to re-start the teams and games which had not been available during the war years 1939–45. You will remember that as a boy I was no good at ball games because of shortsightedness in my right eye. I had refused to wear glasses because of my vanity but changed my mind while in the Merchant Navy when I discovered I could hardly see a whale without squinting and straining. Now as sports master I discovered I was becoming quite enthusiastic and quite adept at games, as I could now see the ball.

After four years I applied to go for teacher training on the advice and approval of the Directors and my fellow masters, as they felt I was naturally gifted for teaching. I was already teaching and having to learn cricket and football, lay pitches, buy sports equipment and clothes, and then coach and play with our teams. We probably held world records for defeating a local team at football by more than 20 goals and another team of cricketers who only scored 5 runs in the first innings and 20 as they followed on to try to reach our total of 140 for 4. Most of our boys were from 13 to 15 years, the other teams were mainly composed of young men, and some of them were over 6 feet tall. Generally they were from local churches.

In September 1953 I started my Teacher Training at St Paul's College, Cheltenham. Ruth and I had by now become deeply in love. She had qualified and was working in a practice in Whiteladies Road, Clifton. We found to our surprise this was the house I had stayed in frequently. Bomber, my cat, was still alive and in the same house! The owner, Ruth's boss, was a former Müller's Boy, Archie Withers, and we knew each other very well as I was the fire-watcher for his block during the 'blitz' on Bristol in 1941.

He was many years my senior, but we had worked together to free people trapped in the A.A. building which had received a direct hit, killing one man and stunning about 12 others taking shelter in the basement.

Our love blossomed through letters. I worked at the orphanage during vacations where I was employed, so we had to use all our free time to get out and about. We became engaged on a farm visit to Kempley, Glos., while staying with Mr and Mrs Carey-Jones, whose daughter was also called Ruth. It was a lovely spot overlooking a patchwork of fields with the Malvern Hills in the purple distance. We chose the ring in a bluebell wood, as Ruth's cousin, a jeweller, had lent me a selection of rings.

My best man and two ushers were from the Christian Union at St Paul's.

We were married at Ruth's church in Bristol and some of her family from N. Ireland and Eire were present. George Harpur, Ruth's cousin by marriage, married us on 21st August 1954. That was the day I left Müller's Homes for the second time. On return from honeymoon, touring Scotland, we lived at No.1 Morley Square, her Aunt Elsie's house. Later this was used as an Elderly People's Home for 26 years. Ruth's father, Mr Robert McMaster, had been a widower since Ruth was six. Her mother, Winnie, had died of cancer and her mother's sister Elsie had brought up Ruth and Jean and cared for their father with the help of her cousin Averil from South Wales. Ruth and Jean were educated at The Park School in Yeovil where they were boarders.

Within four years of marriage we had two children, Alison and Jonathon. Both they and our third child Deborah (born later in the African Bush) brought much fun and laughter into our lives and have continued to do so as we have seen their lives develop and mature.

Soon after Jon's birth, Ruth's Aunt Elsie died suddenly and Ruth's father died shortly after at 94 years. He was 67 when she was born. He died on holiday in Ulster among his own people in Magherafelt. We flew over with the two children, but he had died before we arrived.

Once again we were too late to see Elsie as she died very suddenly when I was expecting we would visit her after school, not knowing the seriousness of her condition. So there we were, left in this rather large house with two little children.

The educational scene was changing in Bristol and new Comprehensives were being built. First they cut down the numbers in the Primary school that I had taught in for three years, and then the Boys' School was to close two years after I'd been transferred. It was then I heard of a need for a trained teacher in Central Africa – so I turned once again to prayer and waiting on God.

Into the Unknown

Once we were convinced that Zambia was the place for us, I gave in my notice at school and we attended the first Wycliffe Language Course to be held in Britain. The course was held in a disused Army Camp and was an intensive six-week course with no spare time. The few children on site were looked after in a crèche, and no one attempted to bring two children along to the course (except ourselves!) but they integrated well and enjoyed themselves. The year was 1959 and it was the hottest summer for many years – good training for missionary work in the tropics.

The ways in which God looked after us financially and in other ways, and the split-second timing of it was amazing and strengthened our faith as we prepared to embark on living by faith.

One incident is worth mentioning: it concerns Ruth's sewing machine. Ruth tells it better than I do. She says, 'It was a Singer but smaller and more expensive than standard ones. Only a few of these machines had been made. Just before leaving for Zambia I took it to Singers to get the motor changed from 240 volts AC to 112 volts DC, only used in remote parts of the world. It would cost quite a bit to rewind the motor, but I felt it was worth the cost as it would be so useful in Zambia. When I went to collect it a few days later the salesman was bursting to tell me something. He said that soon after I left, a strange thing happened. A customer came in with an identical machine to mine. She had come from a remote part of the world and wanted her motor changed from 112 volts DC to 240 volts AC, so instead of rewinding, all he had to do was to swap the two motors and there was nothing to pay. Then he added one more thing. He said,"The other good news is that her motor is newer than yours so you have the added bonus of an almost new motor at no cost." I was intrigued to realise that God could supply our needs even without supplying the money when He chose.'

We left these shores on a cold grey day in November and within a few days of sailing had come through the Bay of Biscay and were enjoying games and swimming on deck in warm sunshine under the blue skies of the Canary Islands. For the moment life was idyllic with good food and fancy dress parties and no hint of the difficult events which lay ahead, too painful and complicated to write here, though not nearly as traumatic as many have experienced on the continent of Africa. We were not going with rose tinted spectacles, we knew too much for that, but we did need this two-week holiday before landing in Cape Town and we gladly soaked it up.

Stepping ashore on a different continent is a fascinating experience, especially in such a beautiful place as the Cape, but after five days we were aboard the train taking us to the interior of the continent. We had to take food on board for the five days that we would be on the train. At first the engine was electrified for the steep ascent up the mountainside to the plateau. Later it changed to a wood burning engine and we were soon covered with black smuts and had to wash our clothes and string them across the carriage. We didn't really mind, as we were so interested in the countries through which we were passing.

Arriving at the Copperbelt town of Ndola, there was no vehicle to meet us as the driver had managed to turn it over in the Bush. We had to buy a car to take us the 350 miles over dirt track to Kalene on the border of Congo and Angola, where there was a mission hospital and the schools that I would be helping to manage. It would be 3½ years and many adventures later before we would return to Britain.

Daughter Debbie with friend Shem in Africa

Lion Attack

A sharp knock on the door of the thatched cottage woke me with a start. We were living with our two young children deep in the Central African Bush in Zambia. I groped for my torch and stumbled out into the passage. Outside the door was an African hospital orderly carrying a message. 'Would George take the hospital car and go to the Jimbe River where a man has hurt his leg.' This was 20 miles through the Bush and the night was very dark. I dressed quickly and went to pick up the Morris Minor open van with the orderly, who spoke good English.

The lady doctors back at the hospital were up and getting things ready to receive the patient. They reckoned we would be back within the hour.

As we set off on the bush road leading to the Angola/Congo border the orderly spoke hesitantly.

'Mr Colletti,' he said, 'this man hurt his leg through being mauled by a lion!'

'Oh,' I said, 'he didn't fall off his bike then?'

'No sir, he was badly bitten.'

That changed the whole picture. Here we were, heading into the deep bush where lions were out hunting. We had no weapons, although I did have access to a rifle.

As we approached the 20-mile peg the path seemed to be swarming with Africans waving their oil-lamps.

Getting out of the cab was a scary business as the darkness of the night closed in. I kept the sidelights on, but they were very small. Out of this crowd emerged two men carrying a blanket tied to a pole. In it was the man who had been carried through the bush from his village. The villagers all seemed to have a reason to come with him.

'We can't take them all sir,' the orderly said. 'We usually only allow his family to come.' We agreed that was the only possible solution to the question, so he chose the man's wife and members of his family. When they were on board, with the patient lying down the centre of the van, and family and baggage arranged each side of him, we tried to set off, but the van was overloaded and would not move as the mudguards were right down on the wheels.

There followed a further sorting out of people, moving one of them into the tiny cab to sit astride the gear lever, which only he could change! The orderly looked to me to give the final word as he had to be careful not to offend anyone – they might put a spell on him!

Very gingerly we made our way back along the dirt track, trying to avoid the potholes, and were soon back at the hospital. Out came the doctors and orderlies and relieved us of the patient. I resisted an invitation to see him into the theatre – I can't stand the sight of blood, though my wife would have jumped at the chance. I made my way back to my wife and family for the few remaining hours of the night. A quick drink and I was soon fast asleep.

Meanwhile, Sahandu was cut free from his blood-soaked clothes and his wounds treated. His wife and family were given a thatched house along with all the other patients' families, so they could cook and care for him once the hospital had him in good shape – that would take a couple of weeks.

Two weeks later, after several visits to Sahandu and his wife, he was discharged and they came to have coffee with us. They looked such a fine young couple, bursting with health, strength and beauty. After the usual greetings, as we sat sipping our coffee, more details emerged. It was two lions that were the trouble, a male and a female. The lioness had been injured in both front paws and so was unable to hunt naturally. She had taken to raiding the villages, killing off sheep and goats. Her mate just shared the spoils.

'I had come upon the carcasses of sheep.' Sahandu's wife interrupted excitedly, 'As I rounded an anthill the lioness came into view. I shouted at her and she fled to join her mate who had already eaten his fill and gone off into the Bush. We women and children ran back to the village shouting loudly.'

The upshot was that the men met to discuss plans to get rid of the lions, as they needed to work in their fields.

They decided that Sahandu would lead the hunting party, and that they would need very strong medicine to protect them. 'So we offered payment to the spirits to guard us and give us good success.

As you know,' he added, 'we are very much afraid of the spirits and also of Nzambi – God.'

'Somebody must have heard you that day,' I said, and they laughed delightedly, as though we were sharing a secret – which we were!

'Next day we men set off along the path,' continued Sahandu, 'singing our hunting songs and trying to scare off evil spirits. All went well until we reached the river. We had gone very carefully, studying the bushes and hiding places that lions use, but we were wrong! The lion had gone up an anthill from the other side and we found that out too late.'

'Was it a big anthill?' I asked. Some of them were 30 feet high in our part and had trees growing out of them.

'Yes, it was, very big,' he replied. 'When we went near the dead goats we went very carefully but never thought to look up! In a split second the lion leapt down onto my right side, knocking me to the ground, and my gun out of my hand.'

'What about your friends?'

'They had scrambled up the nearest trees,' he replied wryly. 'So there I was, down in the dust and the lioness had me in her mouth. She held me down by the neck and legs, my right thigh was in her mouth and I could feel her teeth on my hipbone. She was growling horribly and breathing her hot breath over my body. Then I cried out to Nzambi – God – and strangely enough I heard a voice say, "Grab her by the tongue".'

'That sounds very painful and terrifying,' I said. 'What did you do next?'

'I slid my hand down my right side, which was slippery with blood and saliva, and pushed it right through her teeth onto the root of her tongue. New strength came into me, and holding and twisting her tongue, I pushed myself off the ground with my left arm and somehow managed to throw her off. She was growling with pain and rushed off into the Bush.'

'What about your friends?'

'They came down from the trees and tied up my wounds to stop the bleeding. I was in a state of deep shock and was carried back to the village unconscious.'

Sahandu's wife continued the story. 'We got everything ready, drinks and a messenger with a bicycle to send to the hospital as we needed transport to get us there, and that's how we met you,' she concluded.

Sahandu could not remember much that happened until after the 'sleep-medicine' that the doctors gave him had worn off. Then he found strange things happening. The first few days he couldn't keep awake, though he knew his family were with him. He was given lots of tea to drink but no *walwa* (beer)!

'Sahandu,' I said. 'Do you remember when I came to see you one day. You told me you had discovered that you had escaped from another lion worse than the one that caught you by the anthill?'

'Yes, the hospital teacher told us men about Satan who "goes about like a roaring lion looking for someone to eat"! He said it was written in the Word of God. I asked the elder, Mulopu, who was ill in

the next bed to mine and he explained to me how
Jesus had overcome Satan. He read from the words
of God that Jesus had died for us and came alive
again, so that we could be freed from the lion –
Satan.'

'Had you heard that before?' I asked.

'Yes, we had, when we went to the primary
school in the village,' said his wife Njita. 'But it
didn't seem possible for us. We thought it was only
for white people.'

'Now it suddenly seemed clear,' Sahandu added.
'I began to understand that God loves all people,
and Mulopu taught us to pray to God in the Name
of Jesus. So now when Satan tries to attack me I take
him by the tongue because he is a liar and a
deceiver.'

Professional hunters were sent by the
Government and the lioness was killed. She was
pregnant, they found. The male lion escaped into
the bush.

As we listened to their unfolding story we saw
how the Holy Spirit was teaching them who God is.
He had answered when they cried out to Him and
it showed in what they said and in their whole
change of life and thought. Hunting and fishing
and subsistence farming might be their way of life,
but now they had the words of God and had seen
some of their people living their lives God's way.
They knew by faith that God's Holy Spirit was living in them, and so they set out on a new way of
life. The loss of a few goats was well worth it!

Epilogue

These and other experiences in the African Bush live very vividly in our memories.

Being privileged to help Gordon Suckling in planning and setting up youth camps in Zambia, much on the same lines as Bristol Christian Youth Camps, was something which I enjoyed. Other tasks were not so enjoyable, but certainly constituted a challenge and took all the ingenuity we could muster – carrying patients over a swollen river to reach the hospital (at Kalene) or mending the road with loose stones and branches to make it passable were all in a day's work.

Life was primitive and every day brought the unexpected problems. Basic living meant ensuring a supply of wood, water and food, coping with the elements, the roads (dirt tracks) the electricity generator, heat, illness and disease and often the underlying battle with evil. There was the brighter side also, swimming in the river, laughing with the Lunda people, camping with them by the Zambezi River, and then too, the many answers to prayer, like bursts of sunshine that made us sure that God is who He says He is, and is with us in struggles and difficulties.

I will outline just two of these answers, the first one in Ruth's words. Six months after our arrival we experienced our first Bush Conference. Hundreds of Lunda people came from miles around to the Zambezi River. We camped, not in tents but in grass houses made especially for the five days of camp.

The second day of camp was Alison's fifth birthday and we had no present for her. The night before she had knelt down and asked God for a swimsuit for her doll. I had nothing to make one with. Next day a cyclist came from the village where we lived with food supplies and mail. He handed us a large parcel which had come from England. It had taken months to reach us, by sea, train, bus and finally bicycle. The timing could not have been more precise and of course, inside, amongst other good things, was a doll's swimsuit.

Towards the end of our time there, our health was beginning to deteriorate. We were both ill. I was being treated for amoebic dysentery. Ruth had suffered a profound cerebral anaemia at the time of Debby's birth eight months earlier, so it was considered that we were in need of a break.

We were loaded with luggage for the return journey and on the second day of travelling were expecting to reach the Copperbelt town by lunch time, when a knocking in the engine alerted us to the fact that the big ends were in trouble, and to our dismay we ground to a halt. We tried everything we could think of, without success. The sun was scorching and we knew we had no food and only enough water to mix one feed for the baby. We also knew that the bus only passed there once a week – in three days' time! There was silence for a moment.

The two older children stopped chattering, and then a matter-of-fact voice said, 'Have you prayed yet Dad?' It was Jono and we knew he had identified the next thing to do. So, after asking God to send us help, I felt I had enough faith to fix the steel towrope to the front bumper. The next moment I spotted a small cloud of dust in the distance.

It was a bus! A new bus service had started which went along the only place where the road branched to our part of the route in its 350-mile journey. They fixed the towrope on and made room for Ruth and the family while I steered the car the rest of the way. I arrived covered in red mud from the dirt track. These stories seem, somehow, too good to be true, but that is exactly what happened to us.

So, Ruth and I returned to Bristol with our family after 3½ years in Management of Mission Schools in the Northwest Province of Zambia. We had handed over our primary schools to African education.

During our leave I studied for a year in Bristol University in preparation for our return to Central Africa. I obtained the Advanced Certificate, and the Diploma in Education (both now replaced by B.Ed. and M.Ed.). During that time I had to return to full time teaching, as we were unable to return to Zambia due to family health reasons. Much of my timetable was with remedial education, the humanities and religious education. My university studies were in 'The History and Psychology of Education'. A very mixed bag.

After realising that there was little prospect of our returning to Central Africa, I began to apply for posts more suitable to my experience and qualifications. I had been in childcare and education for nearly 20 years. I applied locally, but found it hard to get advancement. Mr C. Poster, the Headmaster, was quite considerate, but seldom seemed to be willing for 'good' teachers to move on. Who can blame him?

I applied for one post with his knowledge and seeming approval, until he remarked, 'You can apply, but I doubt you'll get this post as my wife has also applied.' I hope this isn't libel, but that is my memory of the interview. Later he told me that there was a post for which he had heartily recommended me, and that I could go for an interview immediately. I could fill in the application later! Then I discovered that he was moving on to another school, and that other members of staff were also moving on. There was a general exodus of staff during that end of the school year of 1968; evidently Shakespeare's observation was accurate: 'There comes a time in the affairs of men which taken at the flood, leads on to victory.'

I became Head of Remedial Education at Speedwell Comprehensive School and also a member of the Religious Education Department for the next six years. In both these Comprehensive schools I organised Christian Union Clubs as I had done in the two primary schools before leaving for Central Africa. Other members of staff and senior Christian students helped when possible.

I tried one last bid for promotion by applying for a lectureship post at Christchurch Training College, Canterbury, Kent. I went to an interview and was short-listed. The senior lecturer, Dr Lumsden, [formerly Head of Primary Education at St Paul's College, Cheltenham] said he would be happy to have me on his team, but it was not to be.

We can say that God has provided for us, both financially and in other ways, during all the years that we have lived without any regular salary. Often in times of illness and trauma He has given us confidence and security by the power and comfort of His Holy Spirit living inside us, and we never want to live without Him.

Stories of how He has provided for us, sometimes in ways which seem almost miraculous, would fill another book, but we are not keen to embark on one just now! Speedwell proved to be my final post in full-time education, as in 1974 I responded to a further call from God to leave teaching and return to full-time Christian service in the housing estates of Lockleaze, Southmead, Lawrence Weston and now Sea Mills in Bristol. (My typist Sue was a pupil and is a resident in Lawrence Weston and I pay tribute to her excellent work.)

In early adult life I obtained my education partly from the University of Life, learning much by experience. I have found also, apart from formal education, that bringing up a family is an education in itself and has enriched my life and Ruth's. Our children have taught us almost as much as we have taught them. We would like them to have appeared more frequently in these pages, but their lives would constitute another story in itself. They are now busy in their own different spheres. Jon chose law, Alison chose graphic design and later psychology and counselling, and Debby chose prison work (working with visitor's children) and later teaching.

Jon and Mary, his wife, presented us with two lovely grandchildren, Laura and Robbie, who are now in their mid and late teens. So I find that God sets the lonely in families (Psalm 68:6), as He did for me and as He has done for so many of the children brought up in the Müller family.

George in 1996 – still at work!